Aniville Magazine #2
Cosplayer – Leva Bates

Photography by Jason Koba

Aniville High School Class of 2016

Sound Impressions LLC – Boonton, NJ
Copyright 2016 All Rights Reserved
SIP-0018

For information about custom editions, special sales, signings, premium, and corporate purchases please contact:

Publisher: Sound Impressions LLC

Address: Sound Impressions LLC
                Attn: Publishing
                PO Box 754
                Boonton, NJ 07005

Phone: (973) – 263 – 0521

Web: http://www.storystick.com

Produced By: Jason Koba

Photography by: Jason Koba

Model: Leva Bates

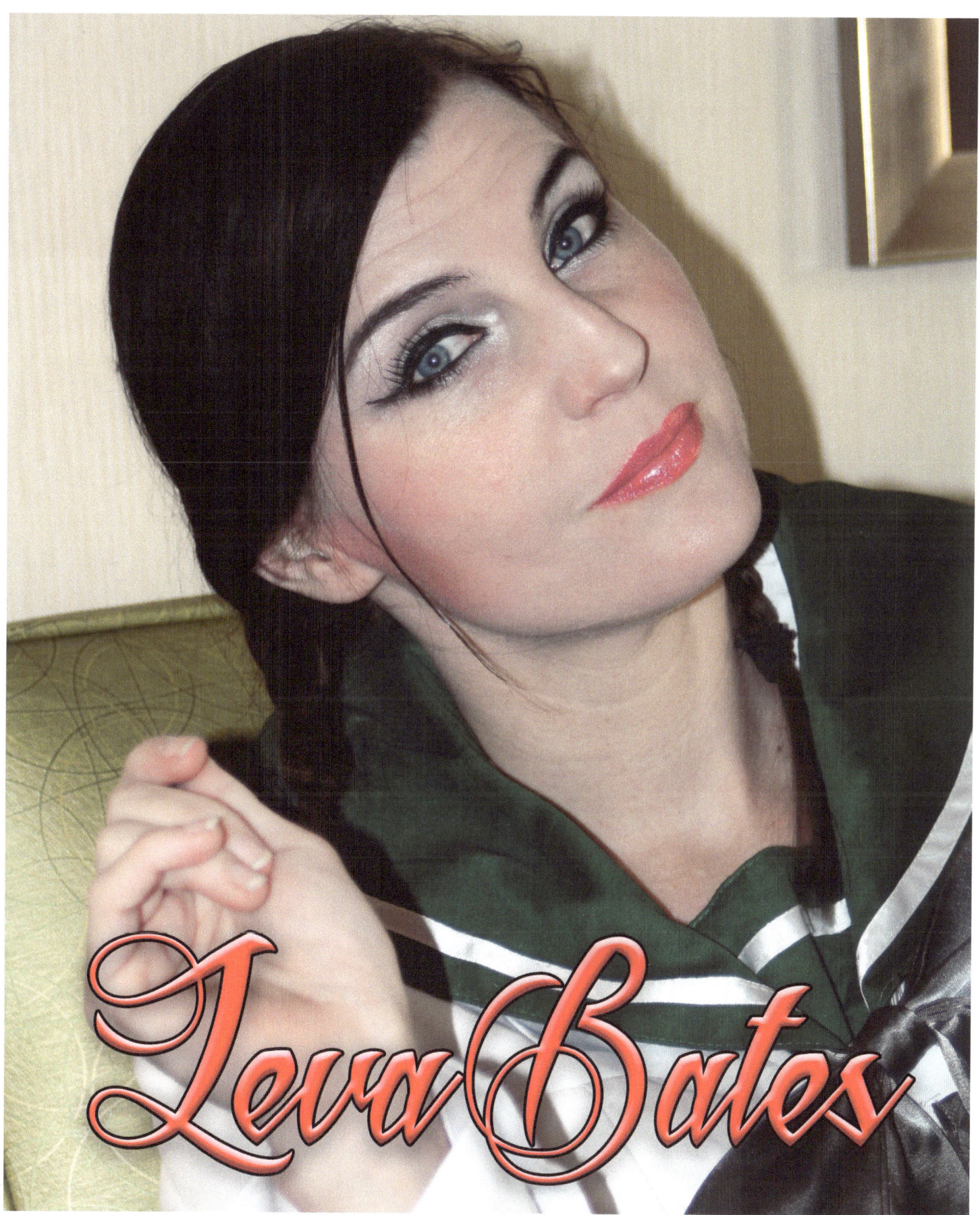

Memories: Sneaking into school late, Waiting for the Principal, Gaming at Recess, and the day of the dead.

Likes: Crossbows, Smashing a Zombie head, Bezerking, The Perfect Headshot

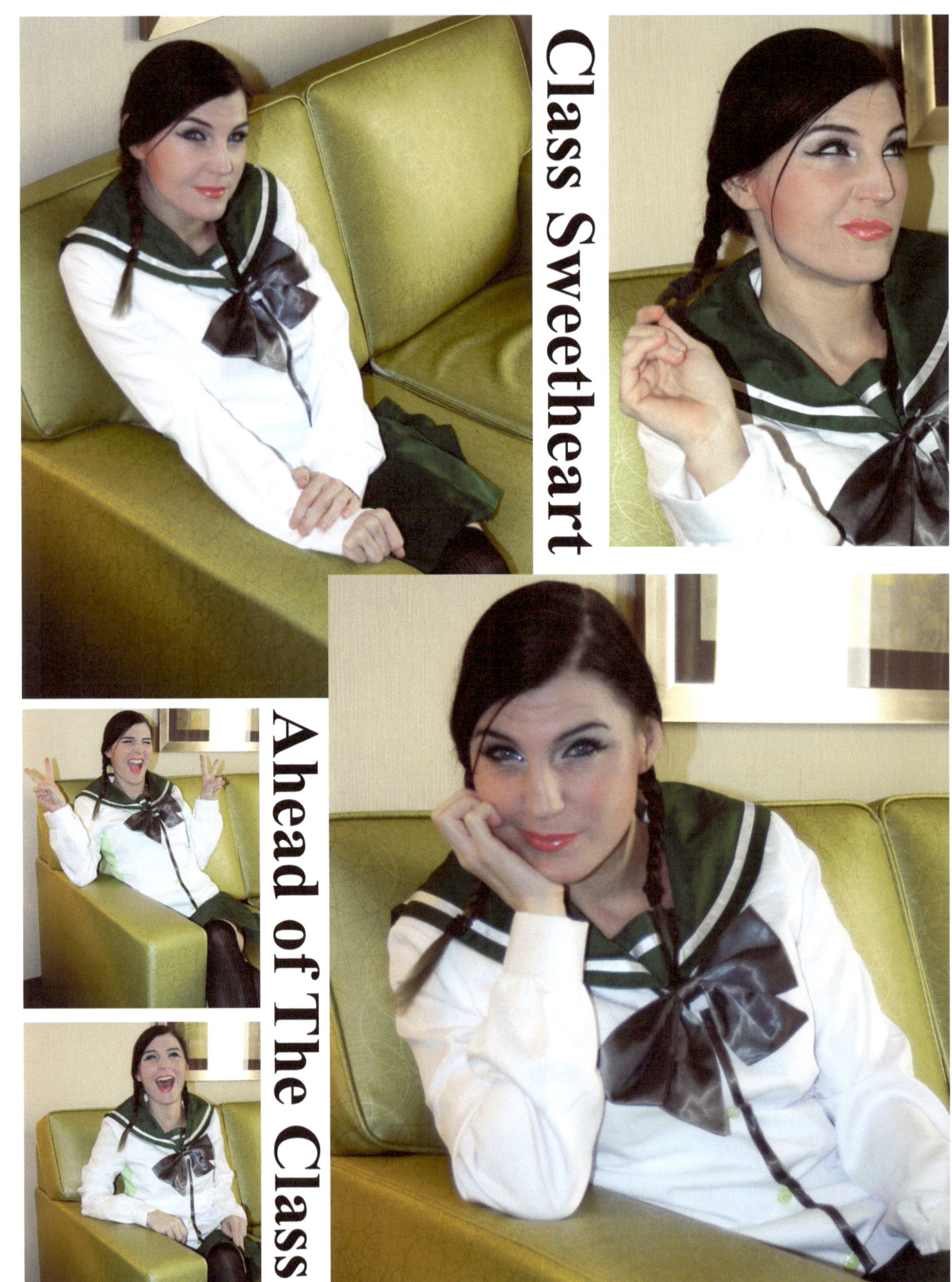

Class Sweetheart

Ahead of The Class

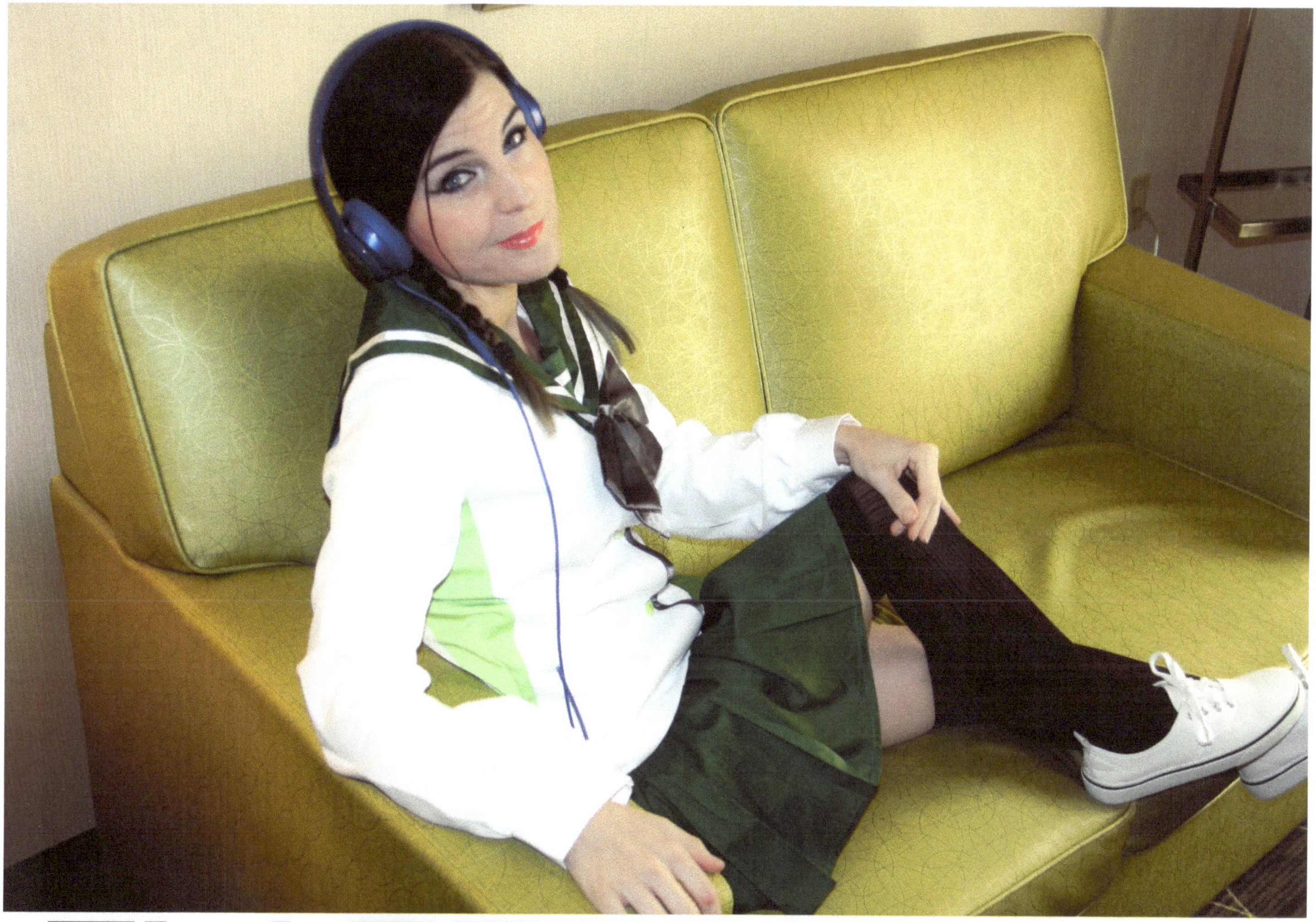

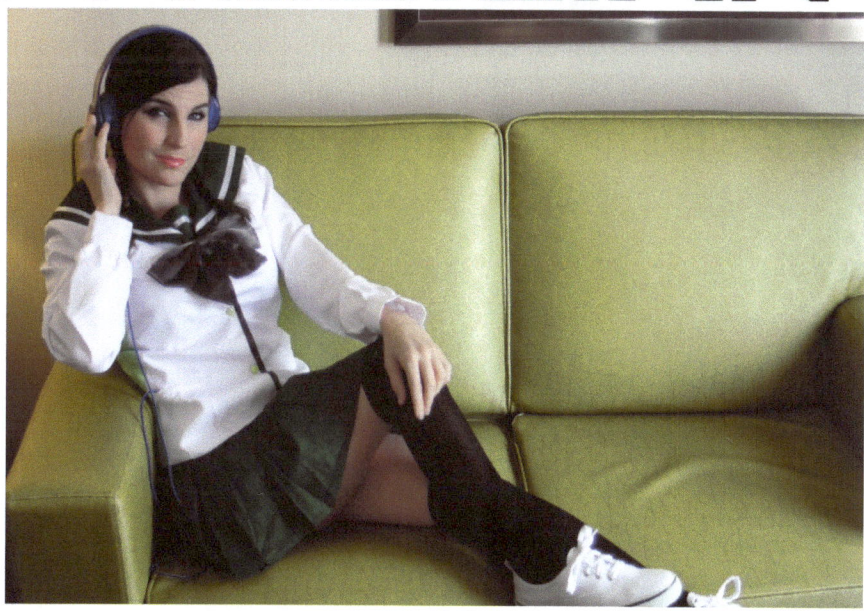

CLASS MUSICIAN

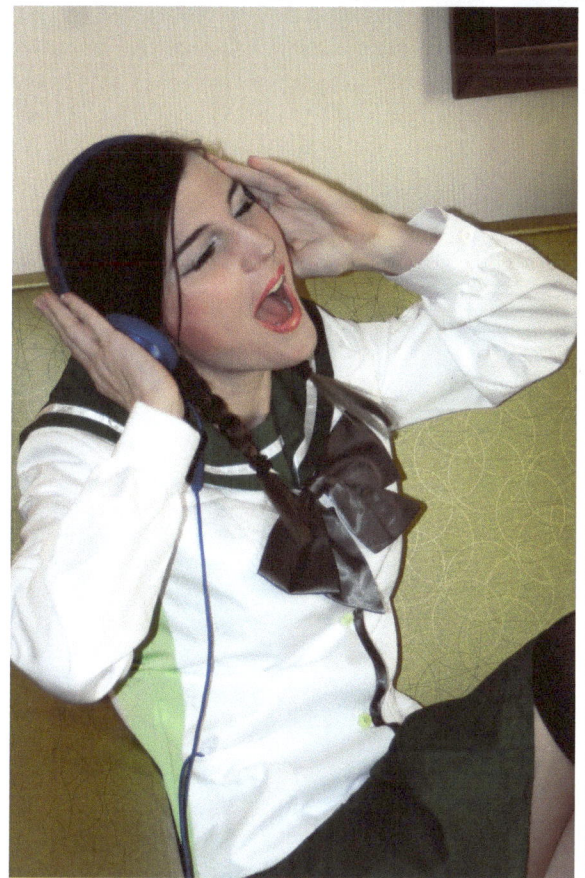

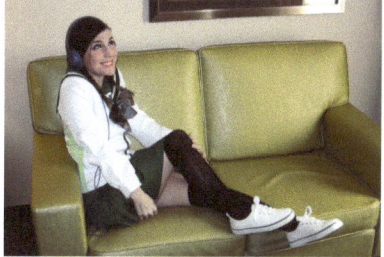

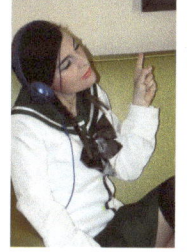

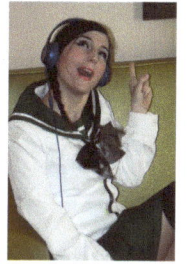

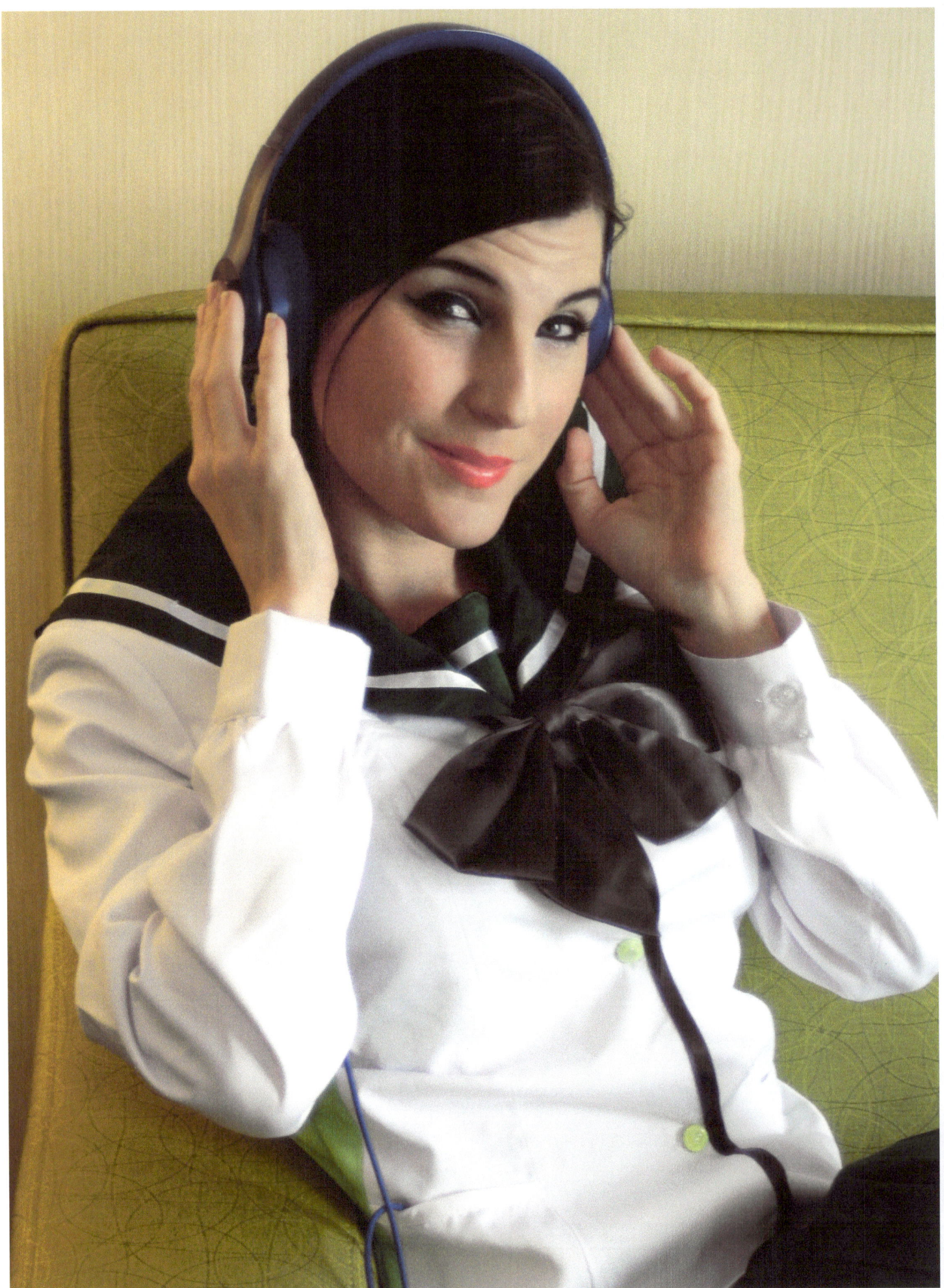

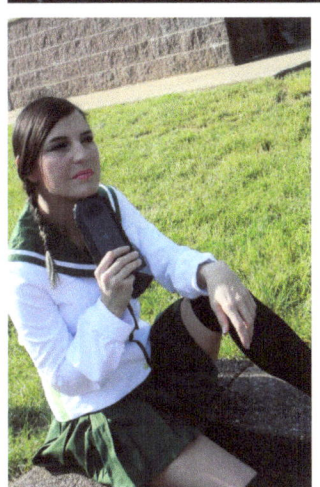
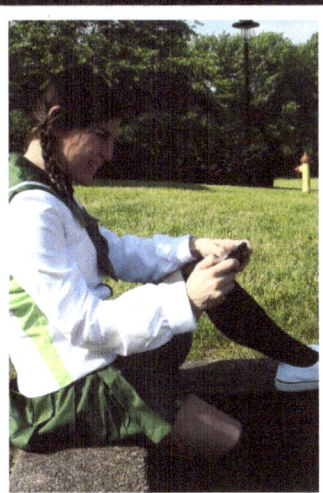
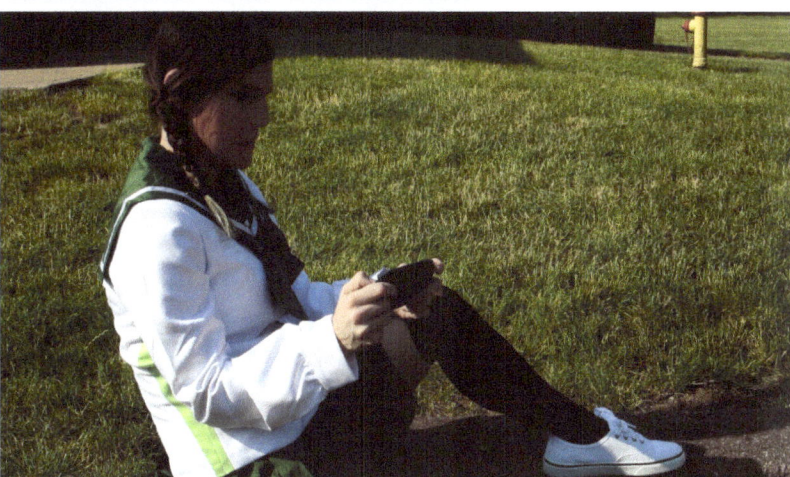

CLASS PLAYER

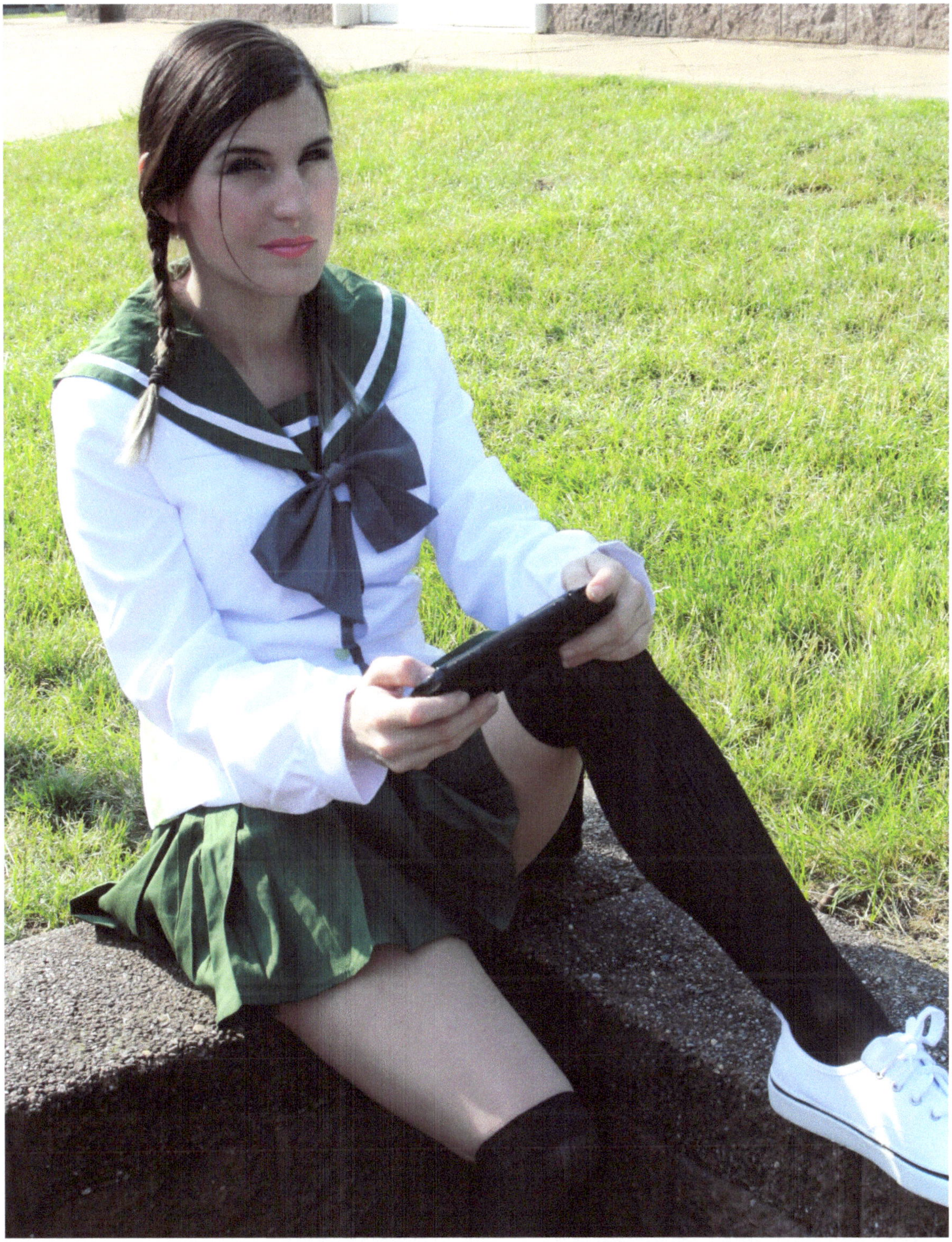

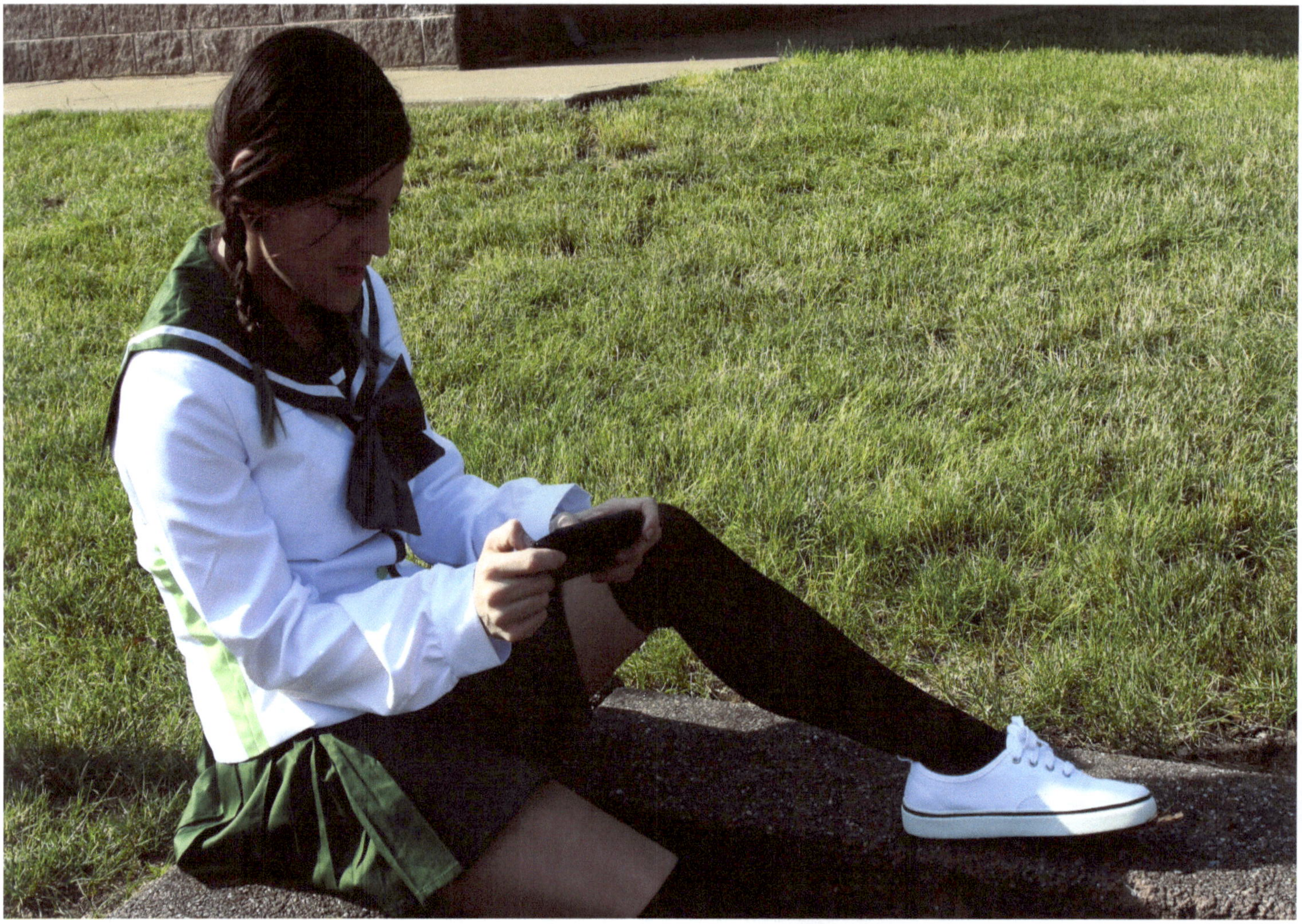

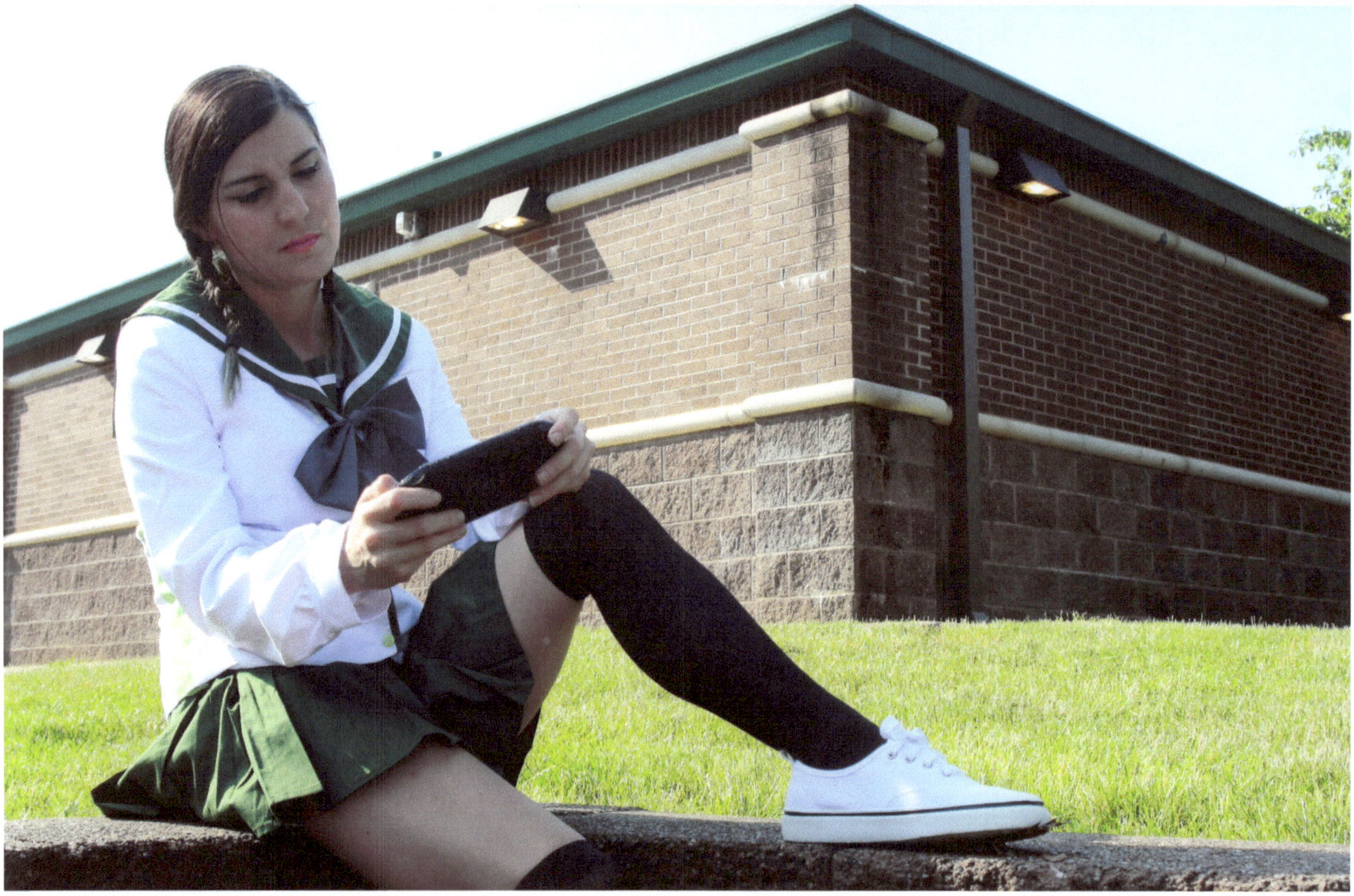

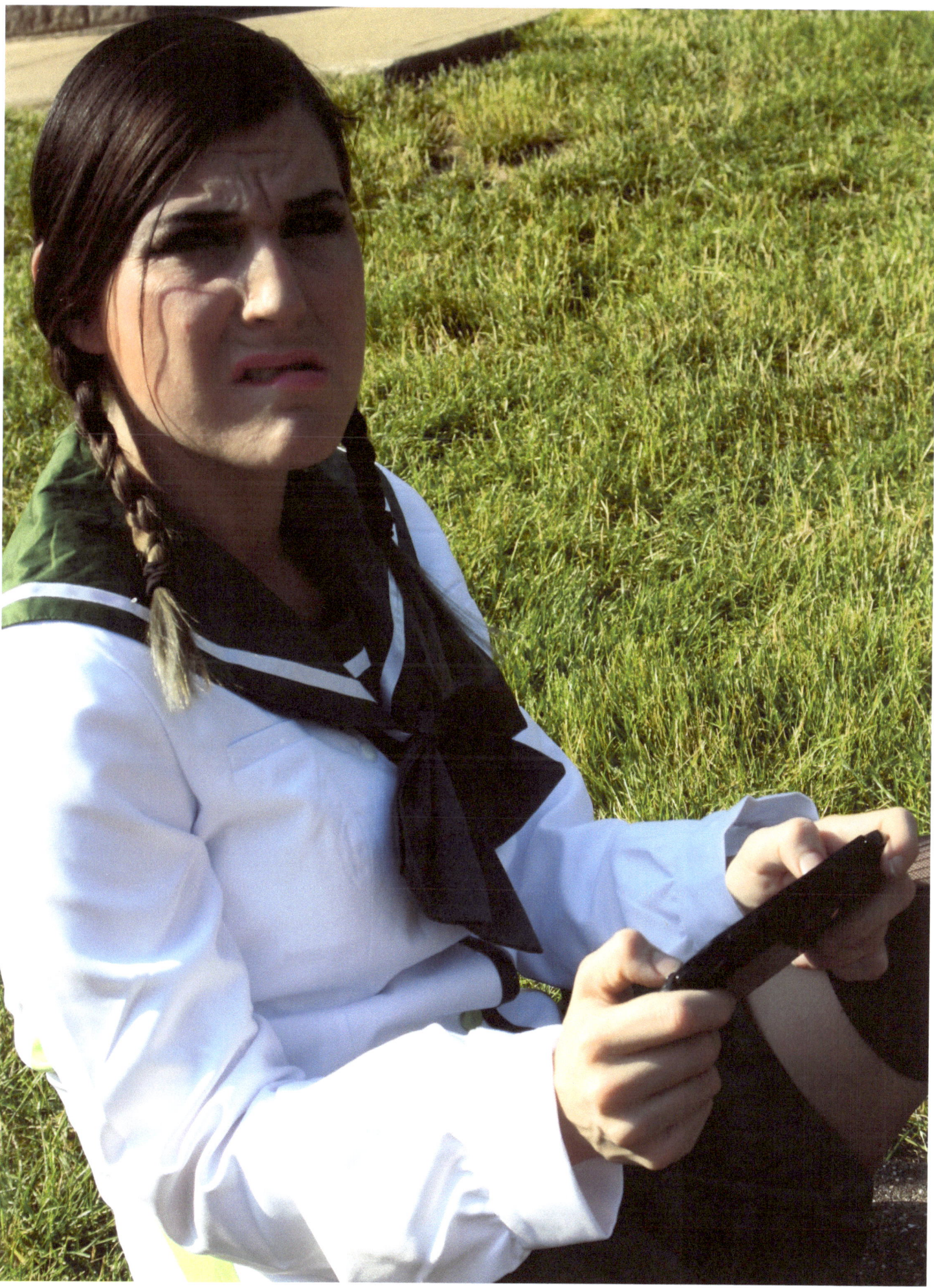

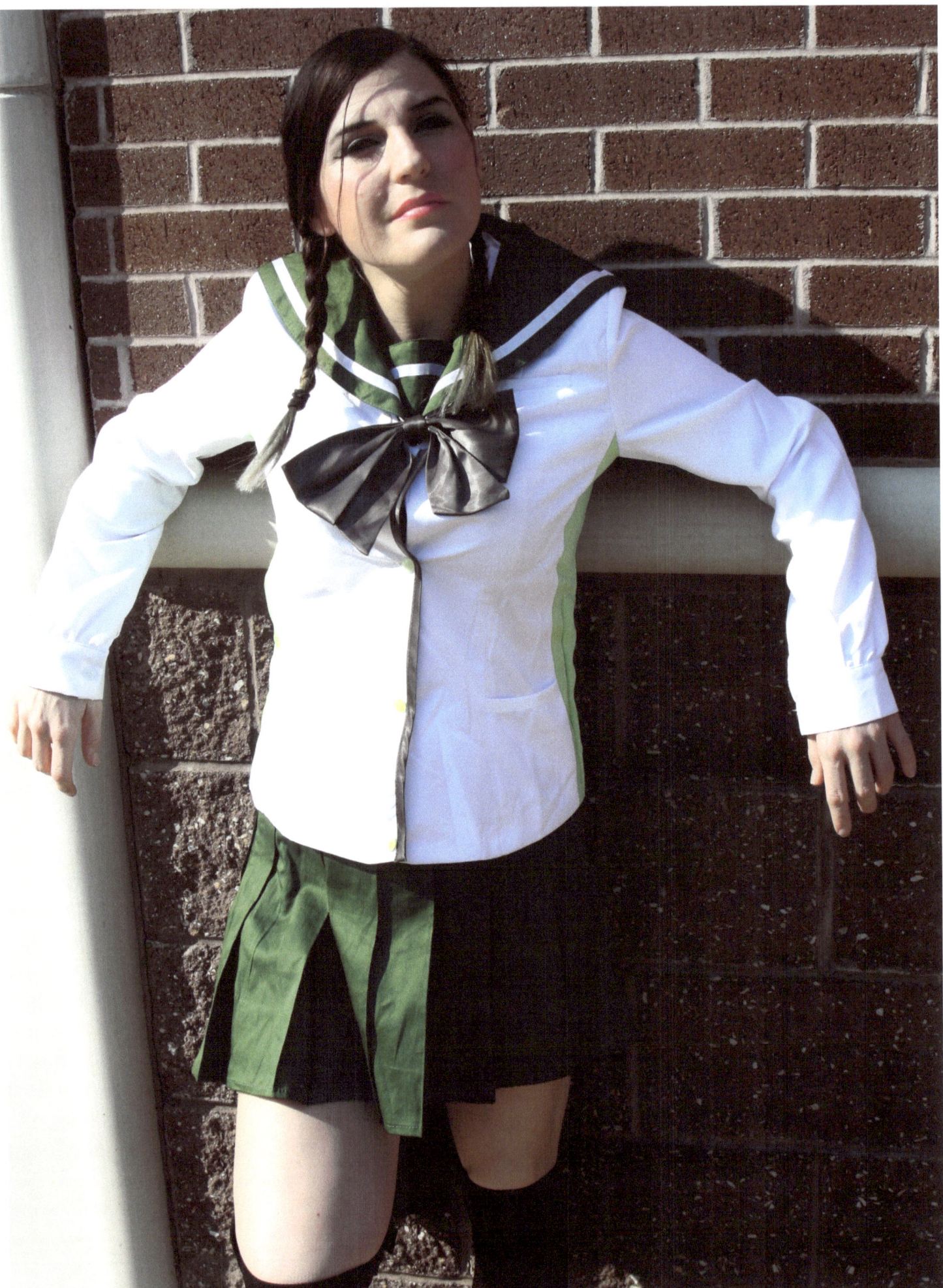

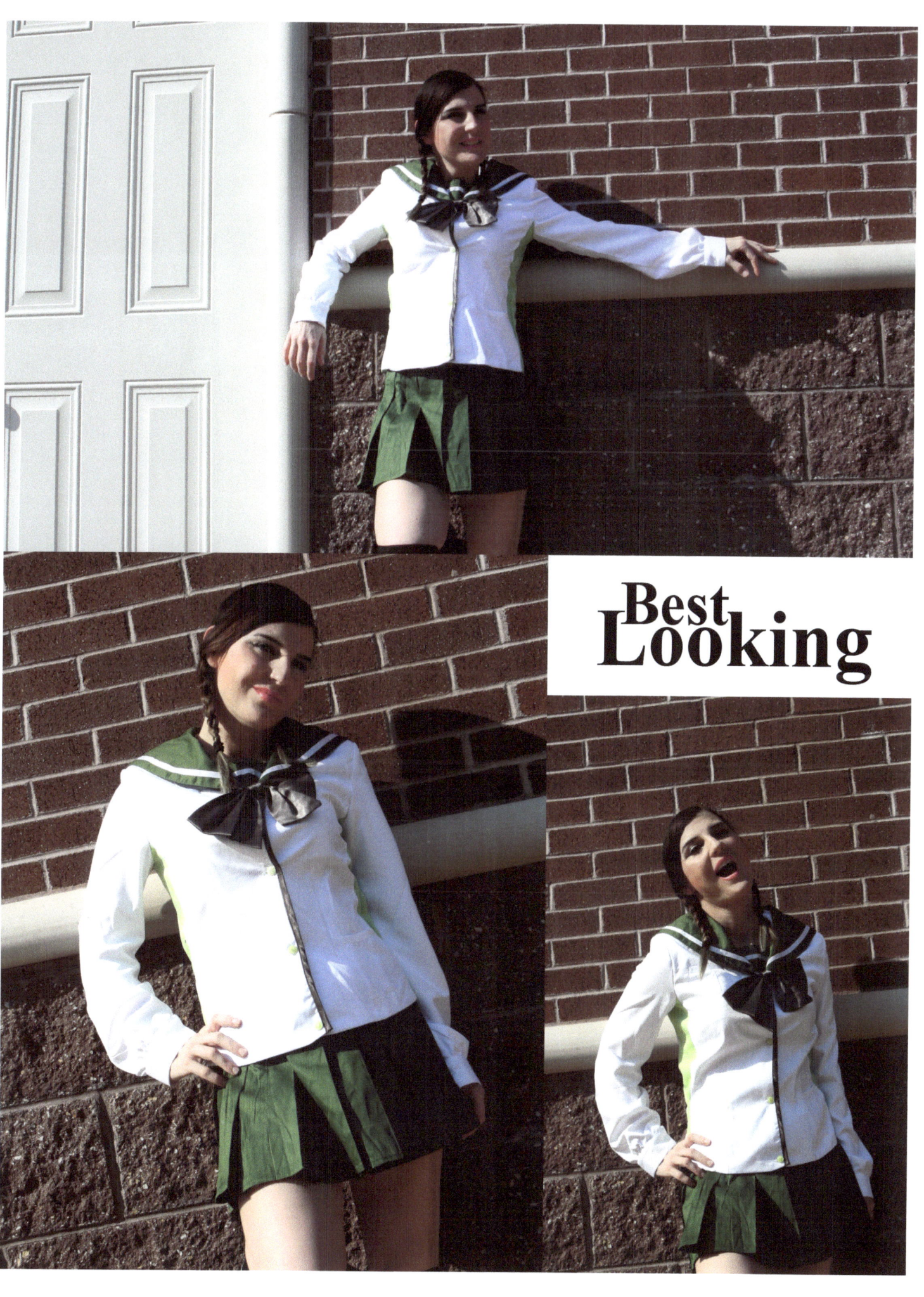

Best
Looking

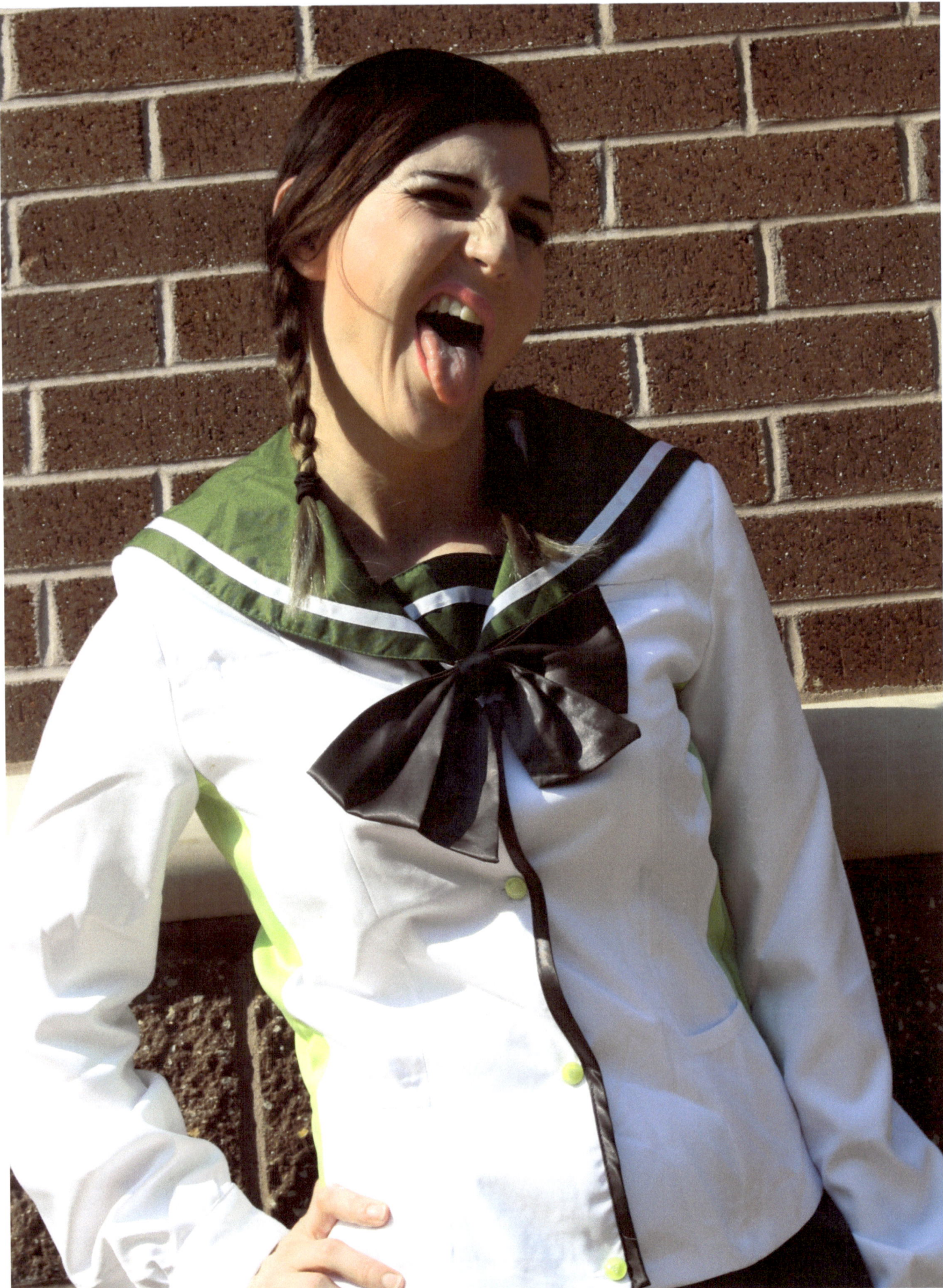

Class Clown

Photographer Jason Koba

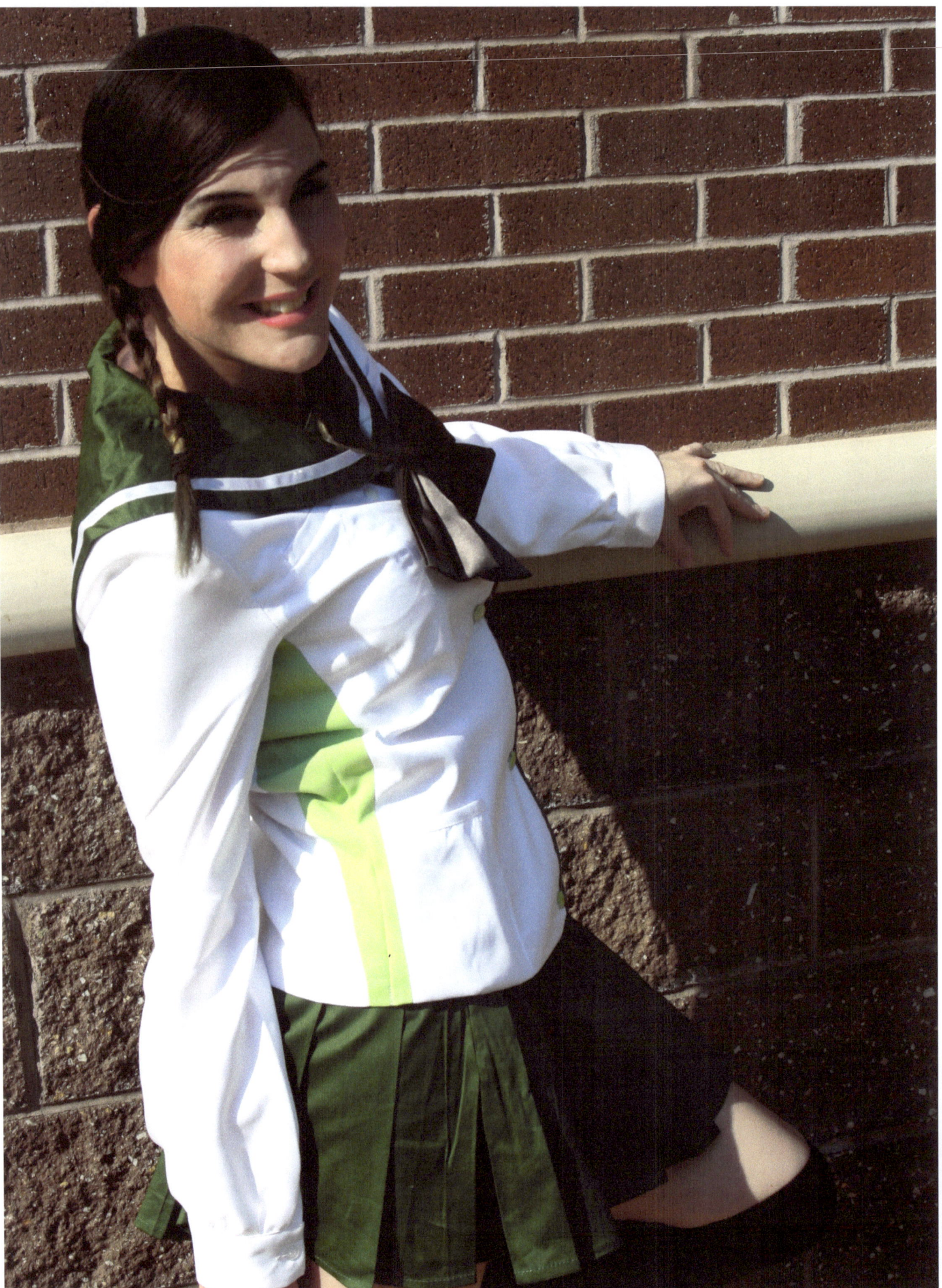

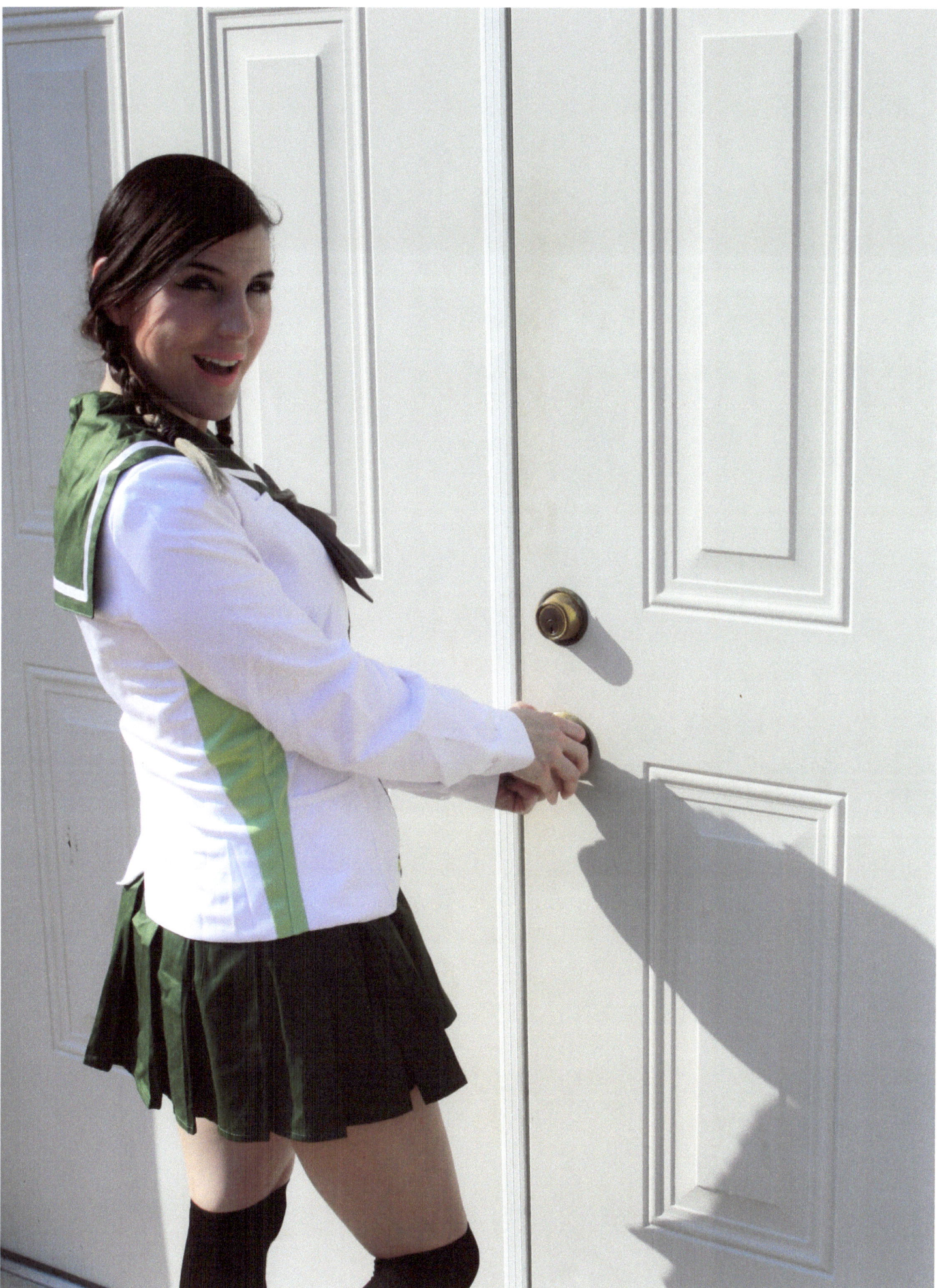

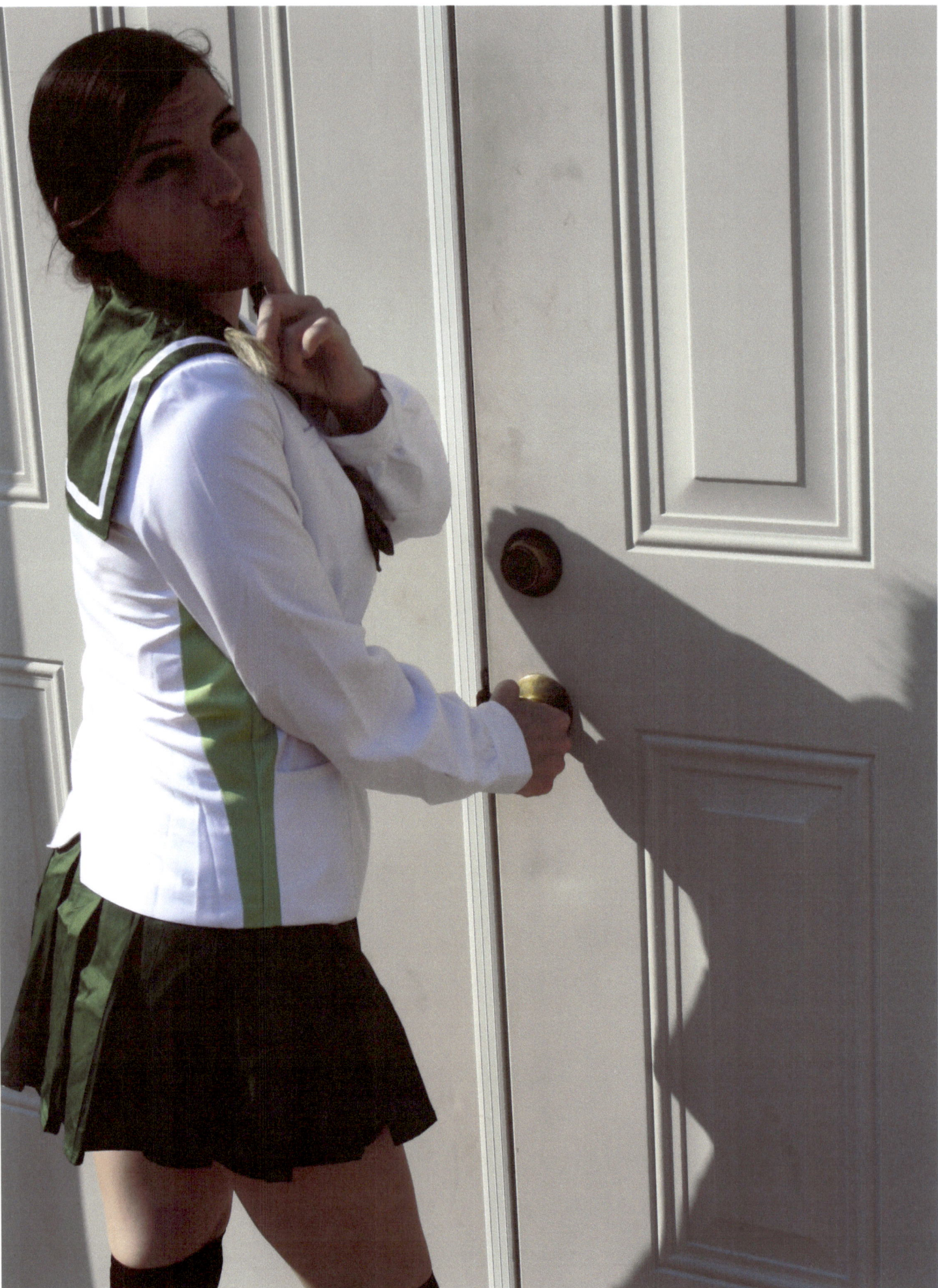

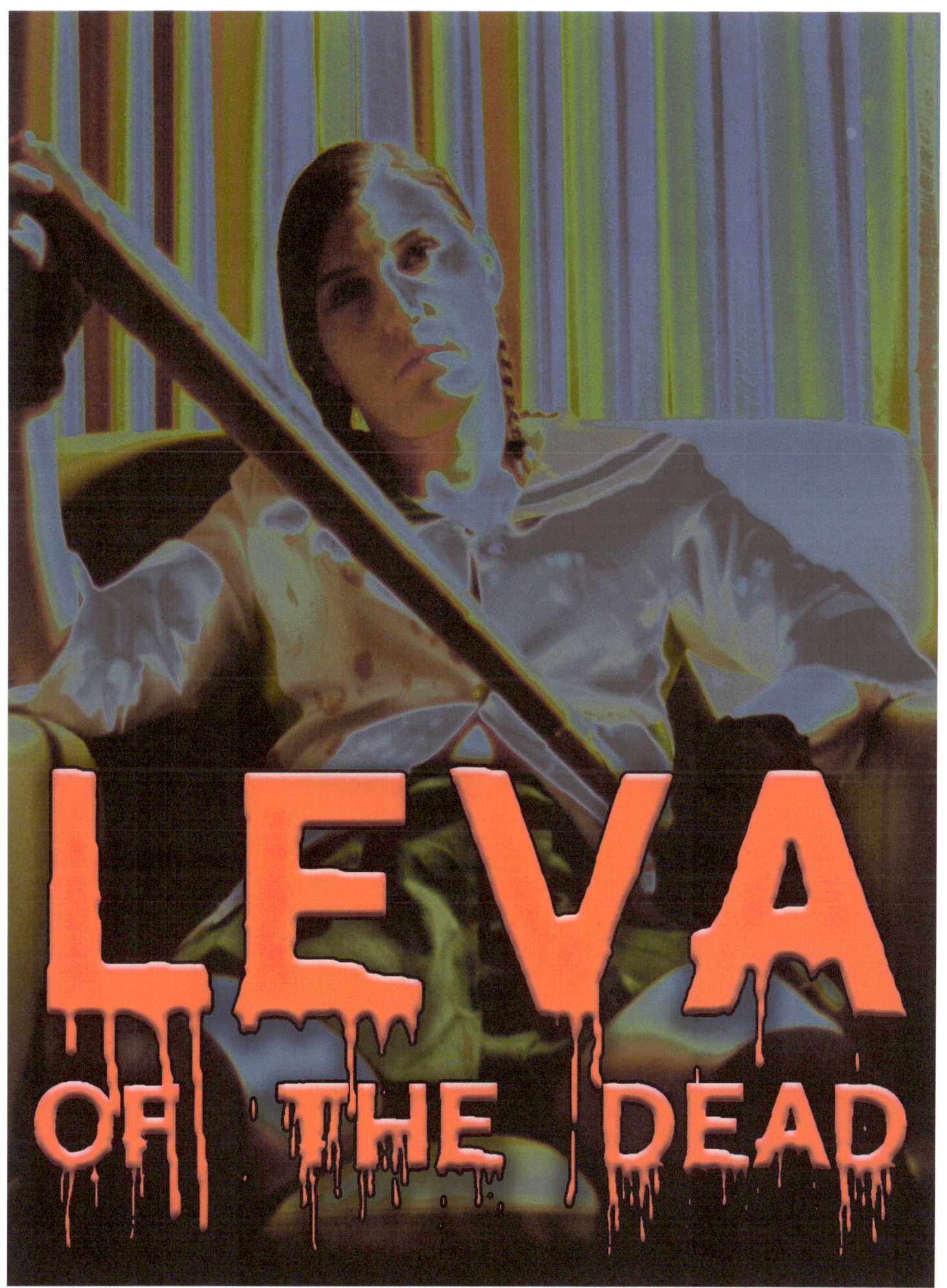

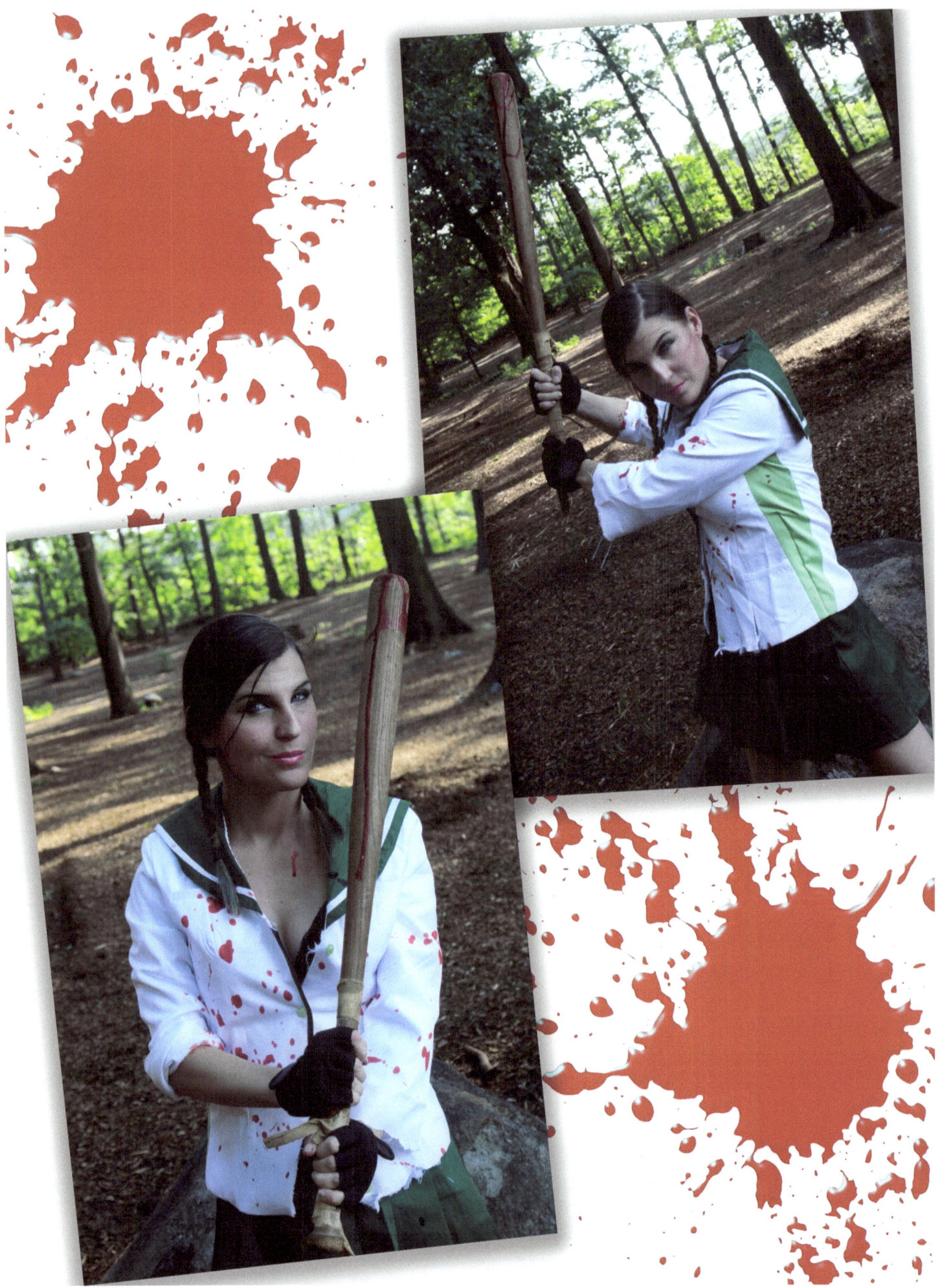

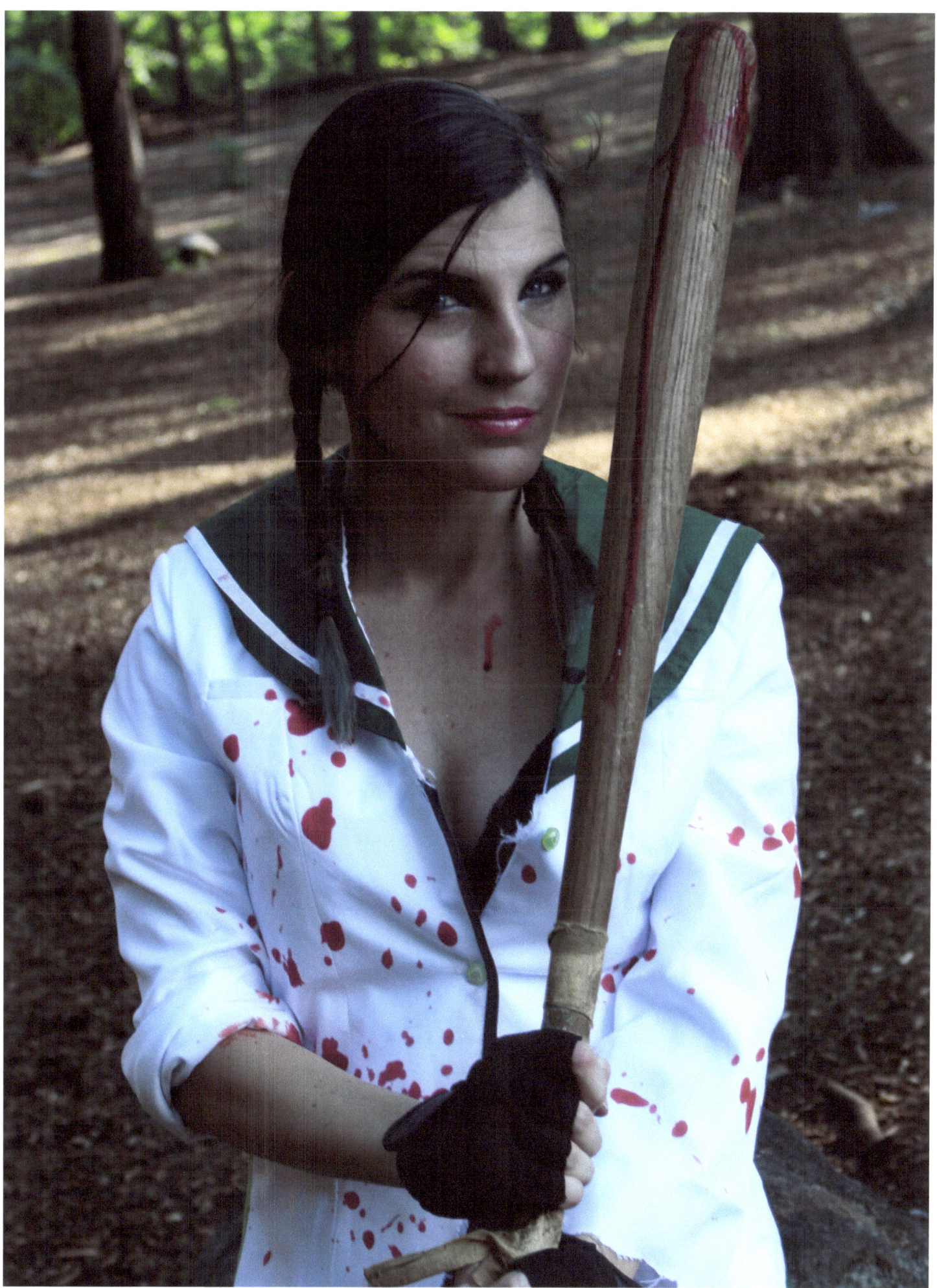

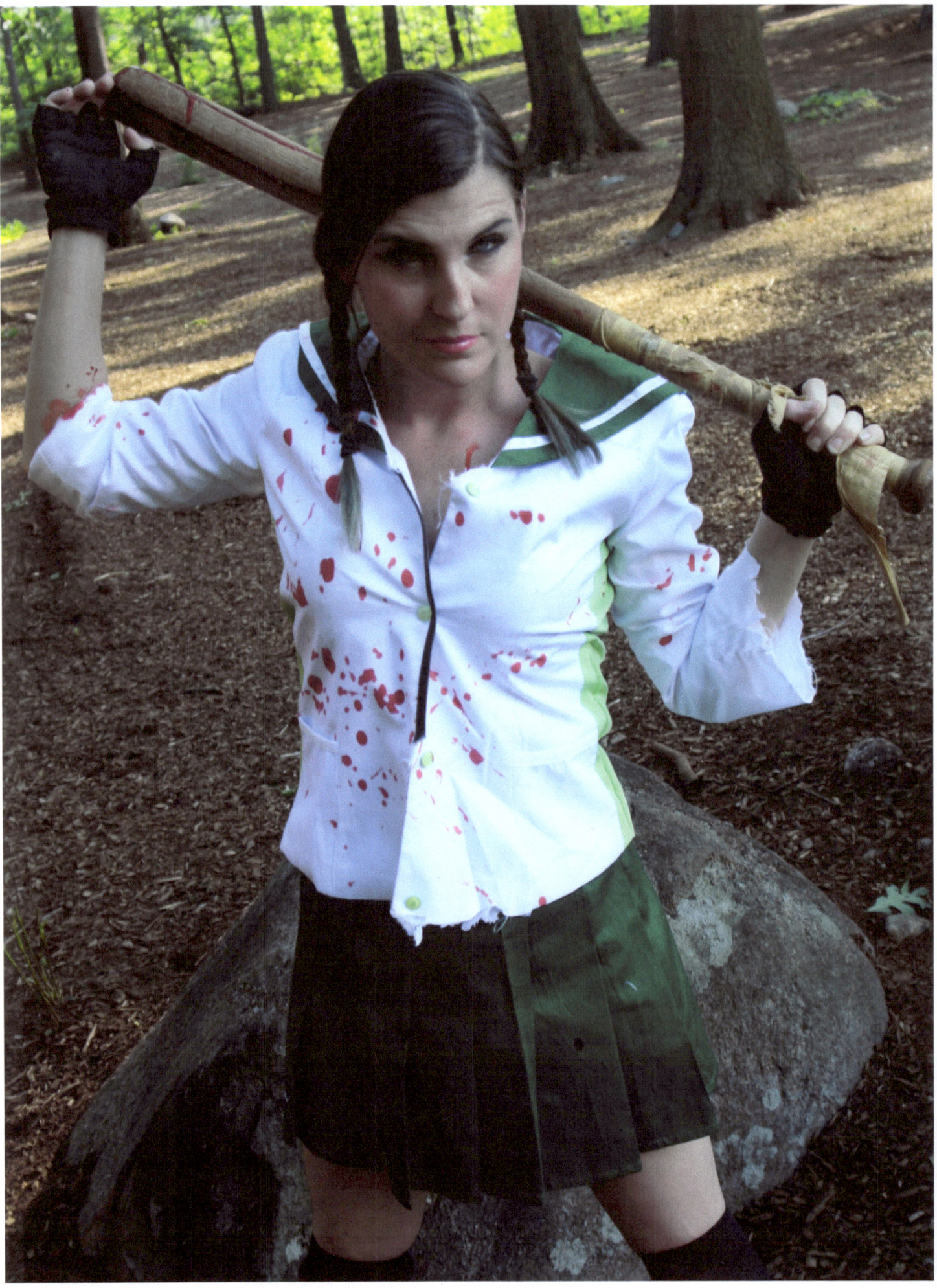

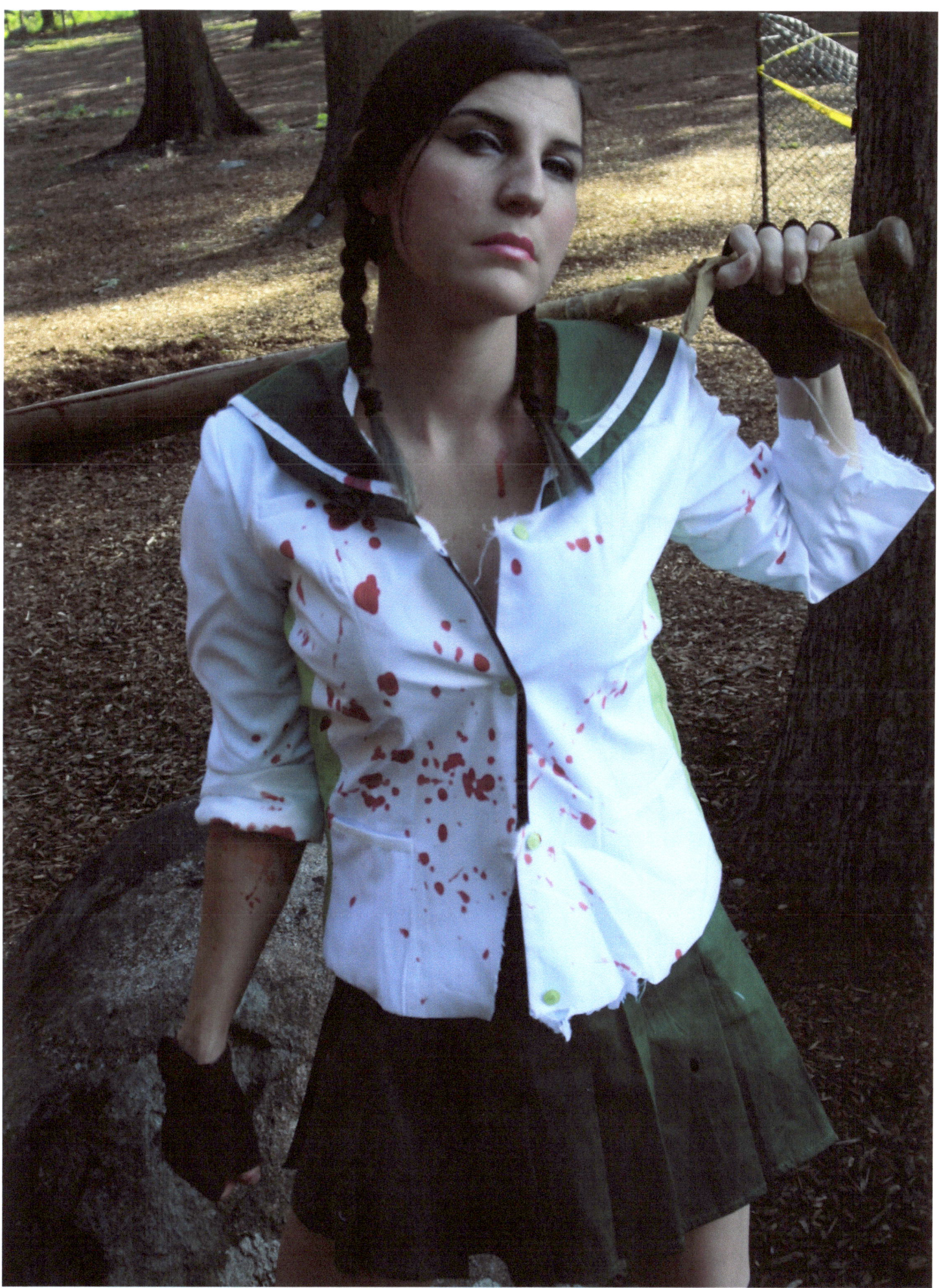

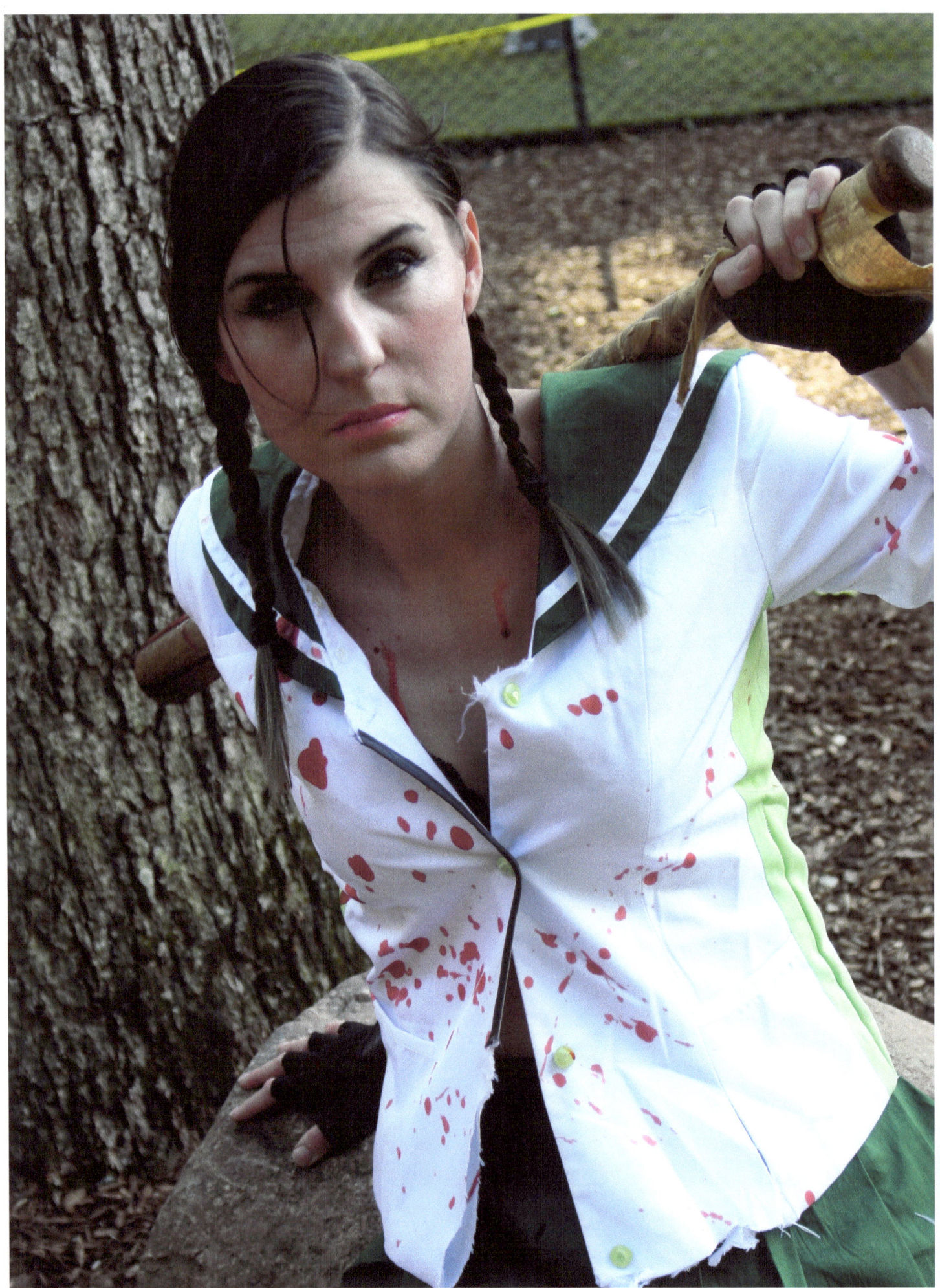

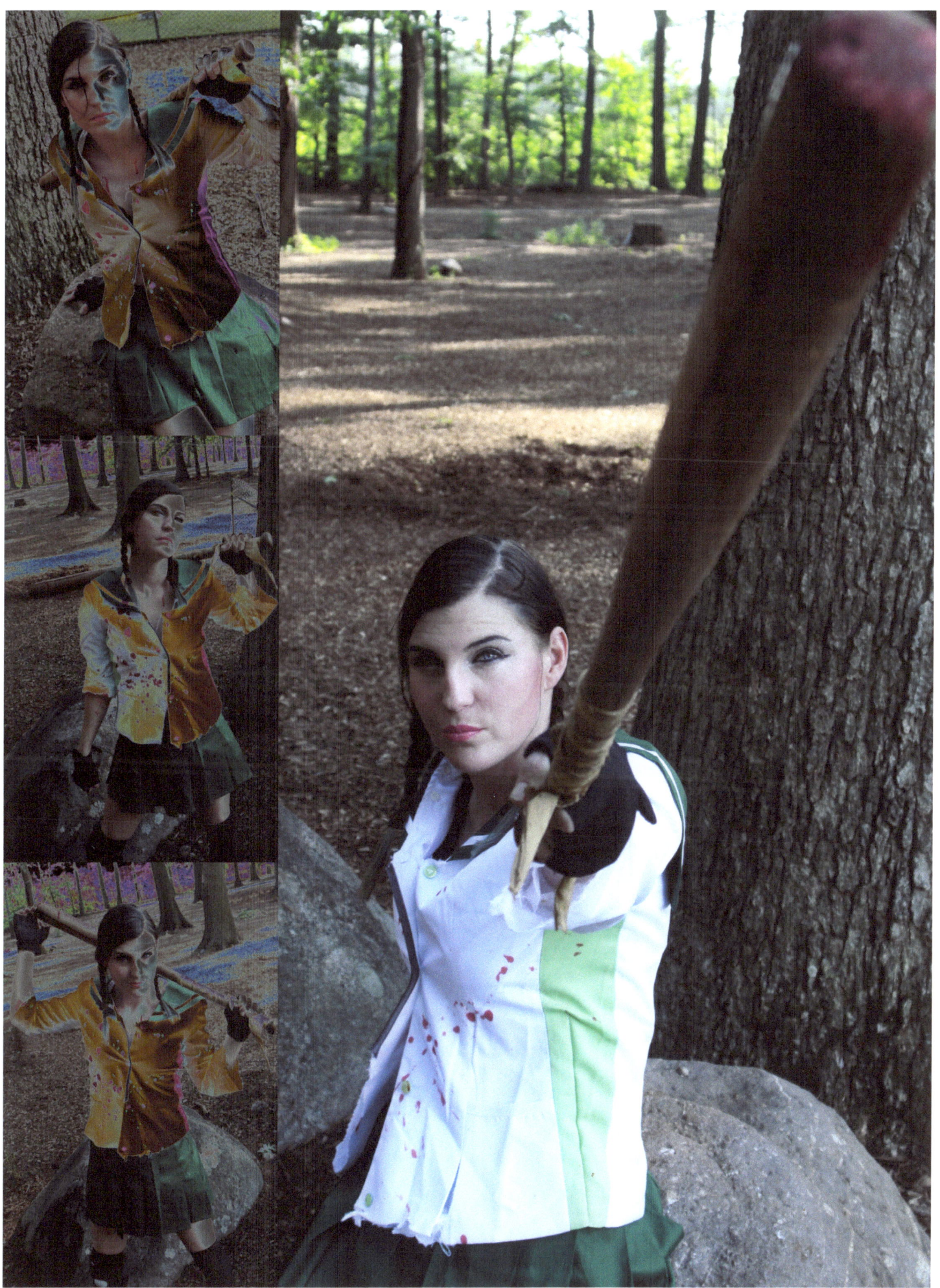

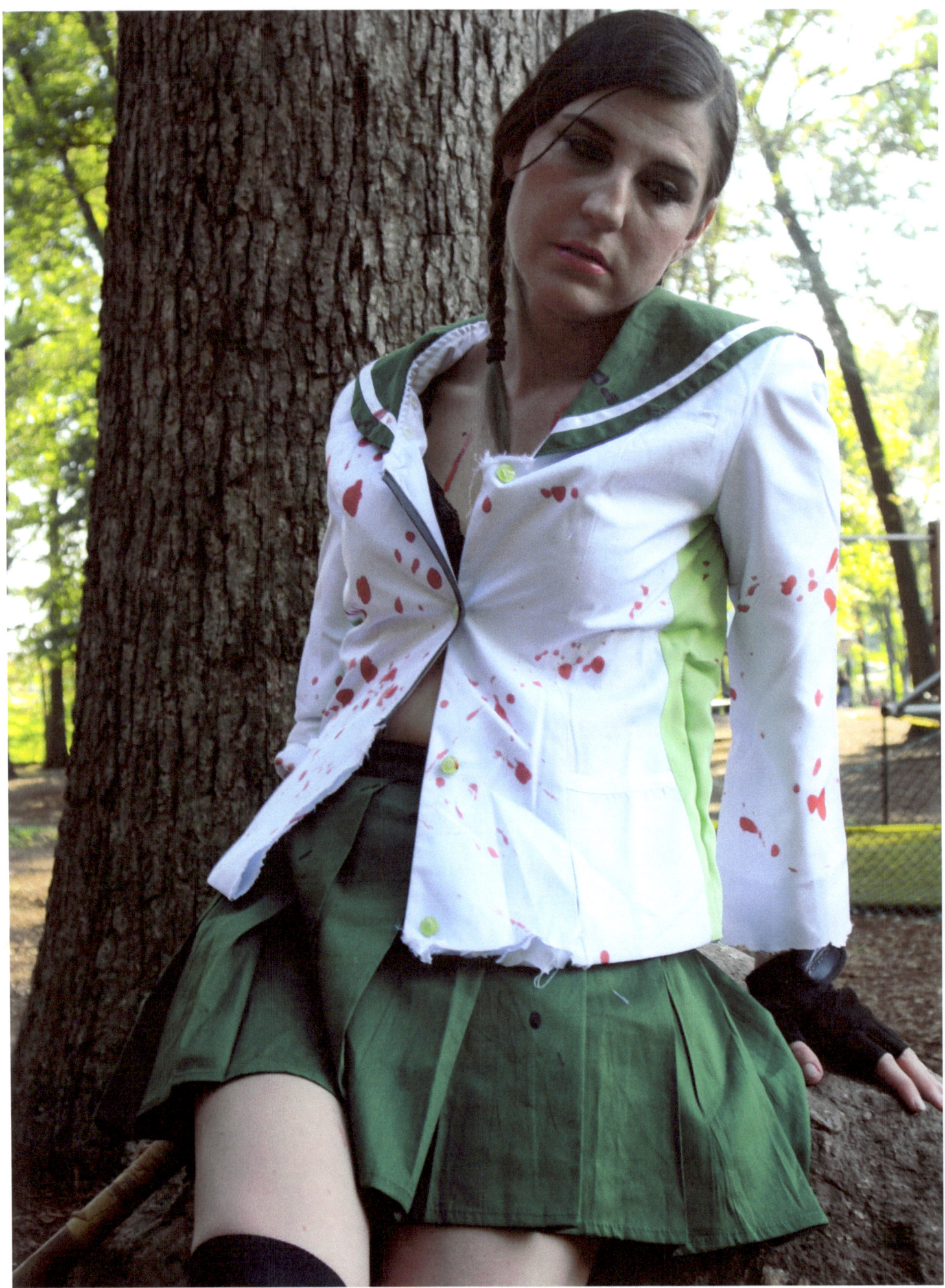

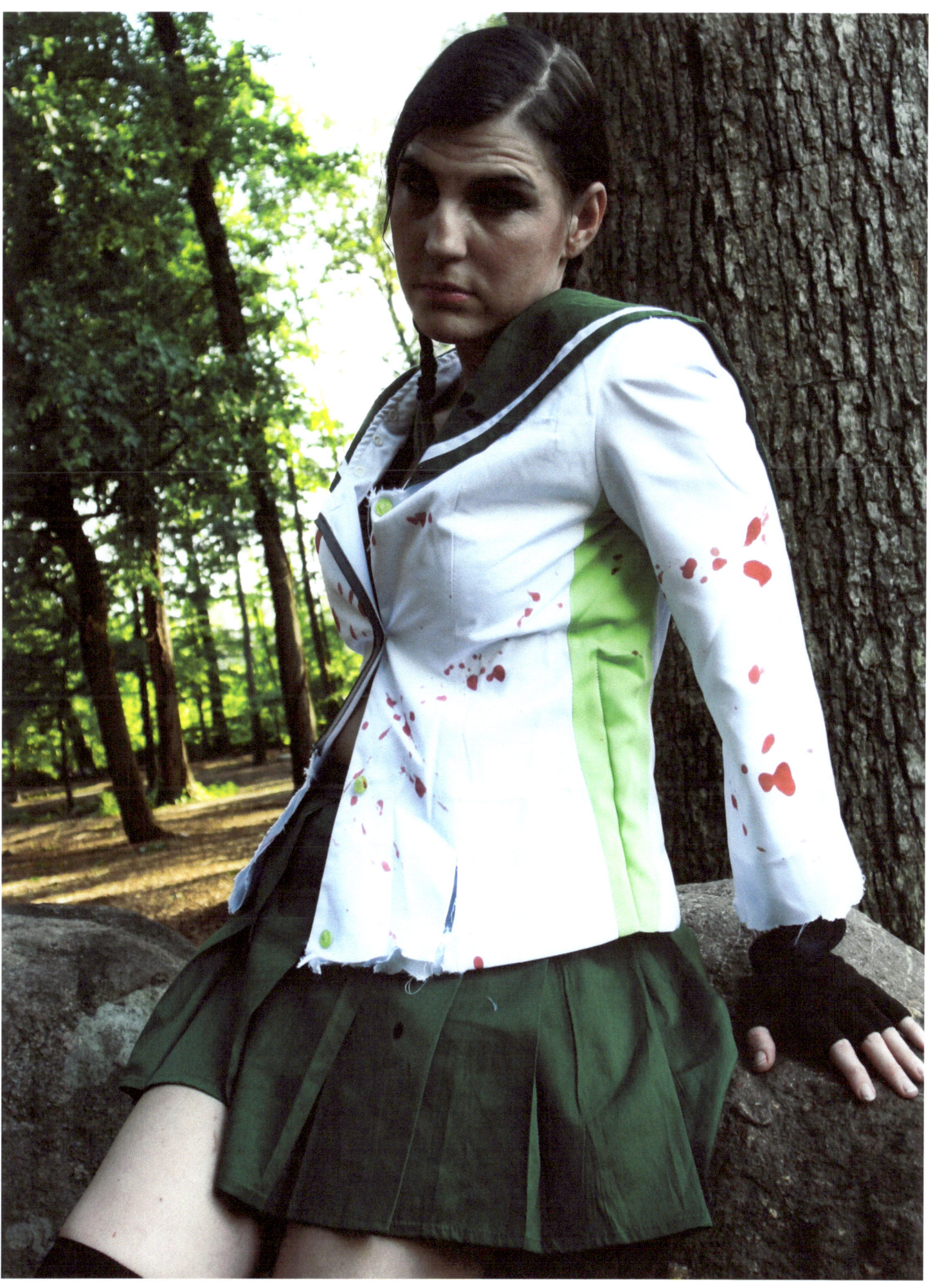

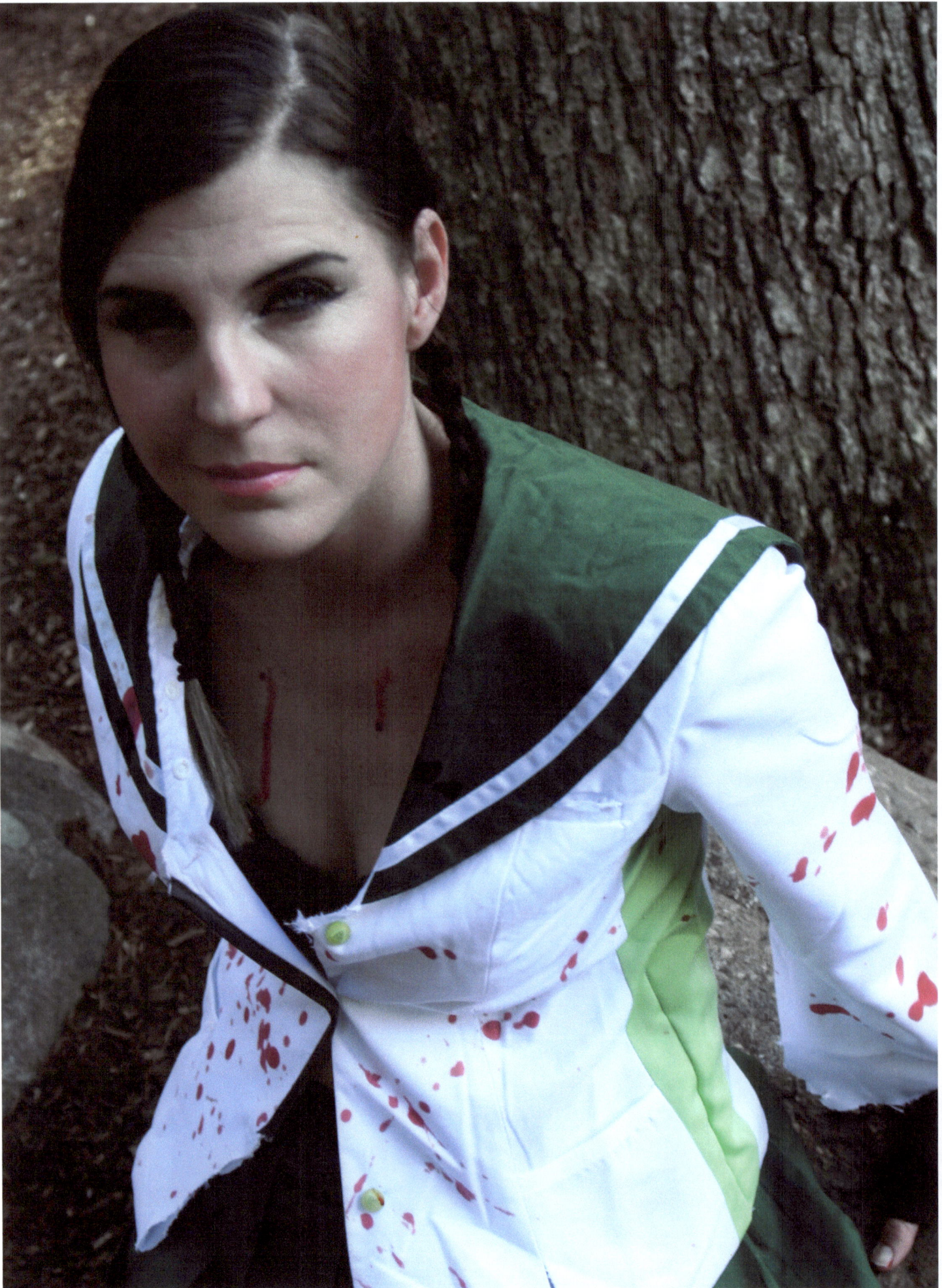

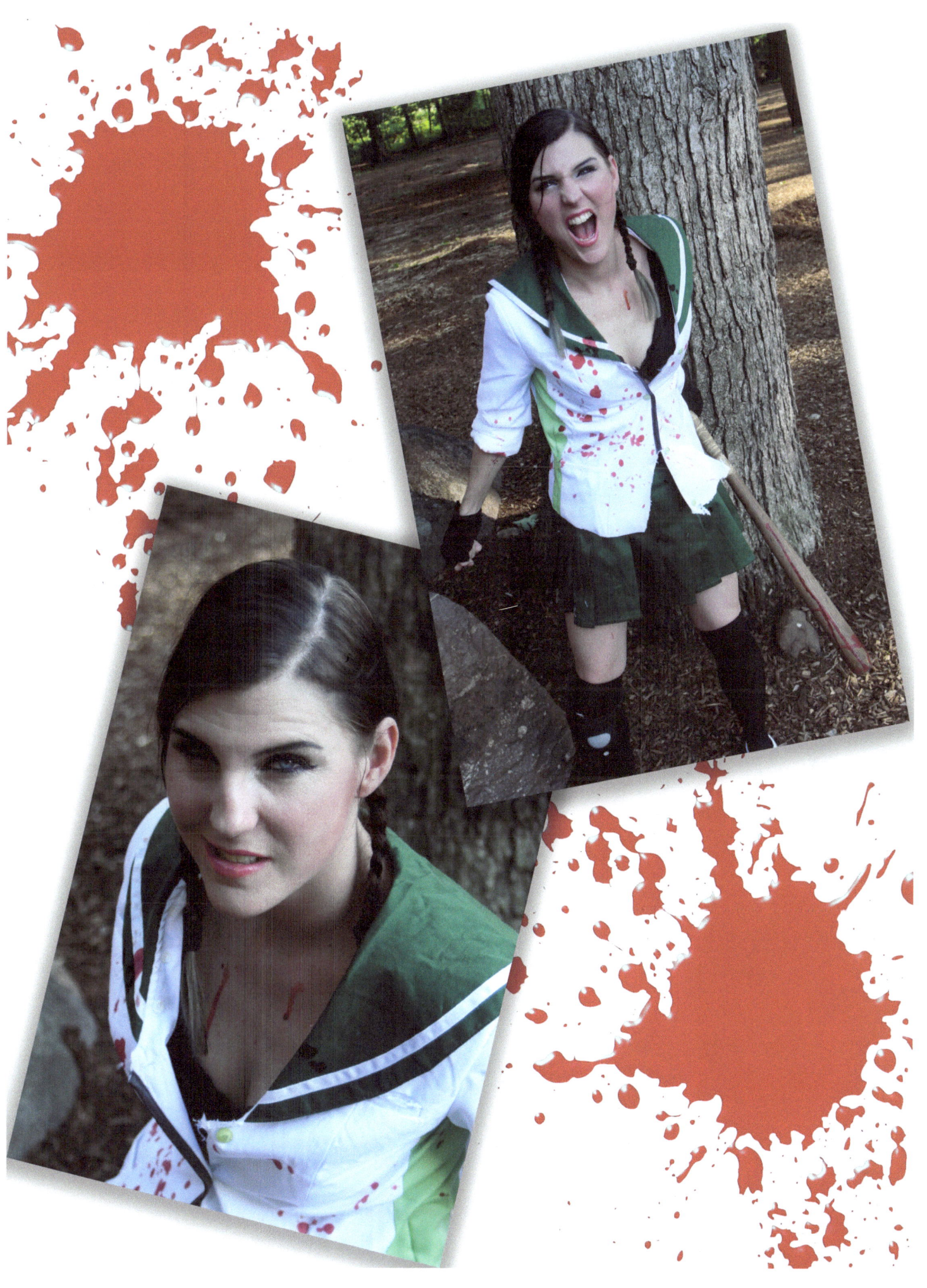

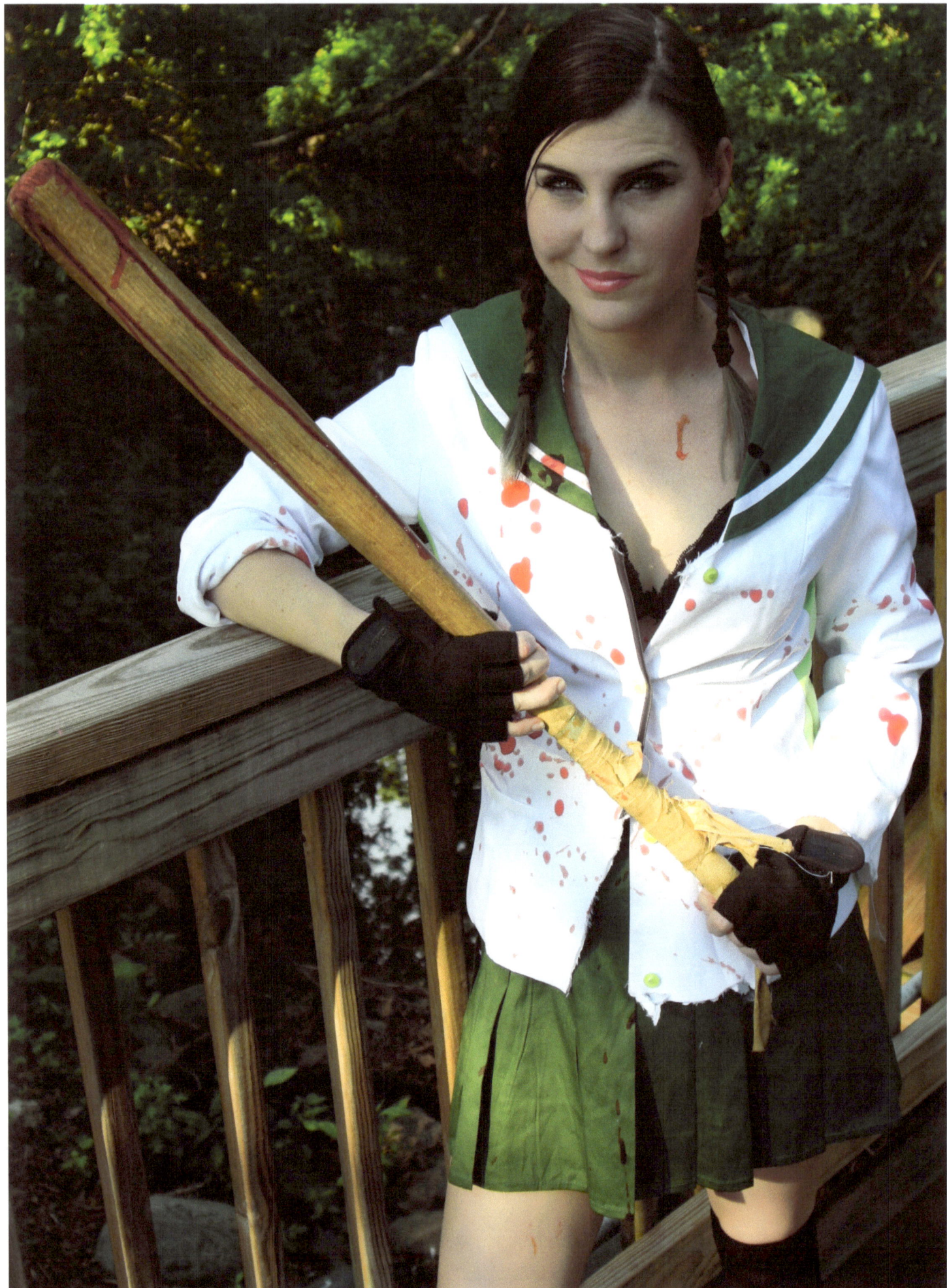

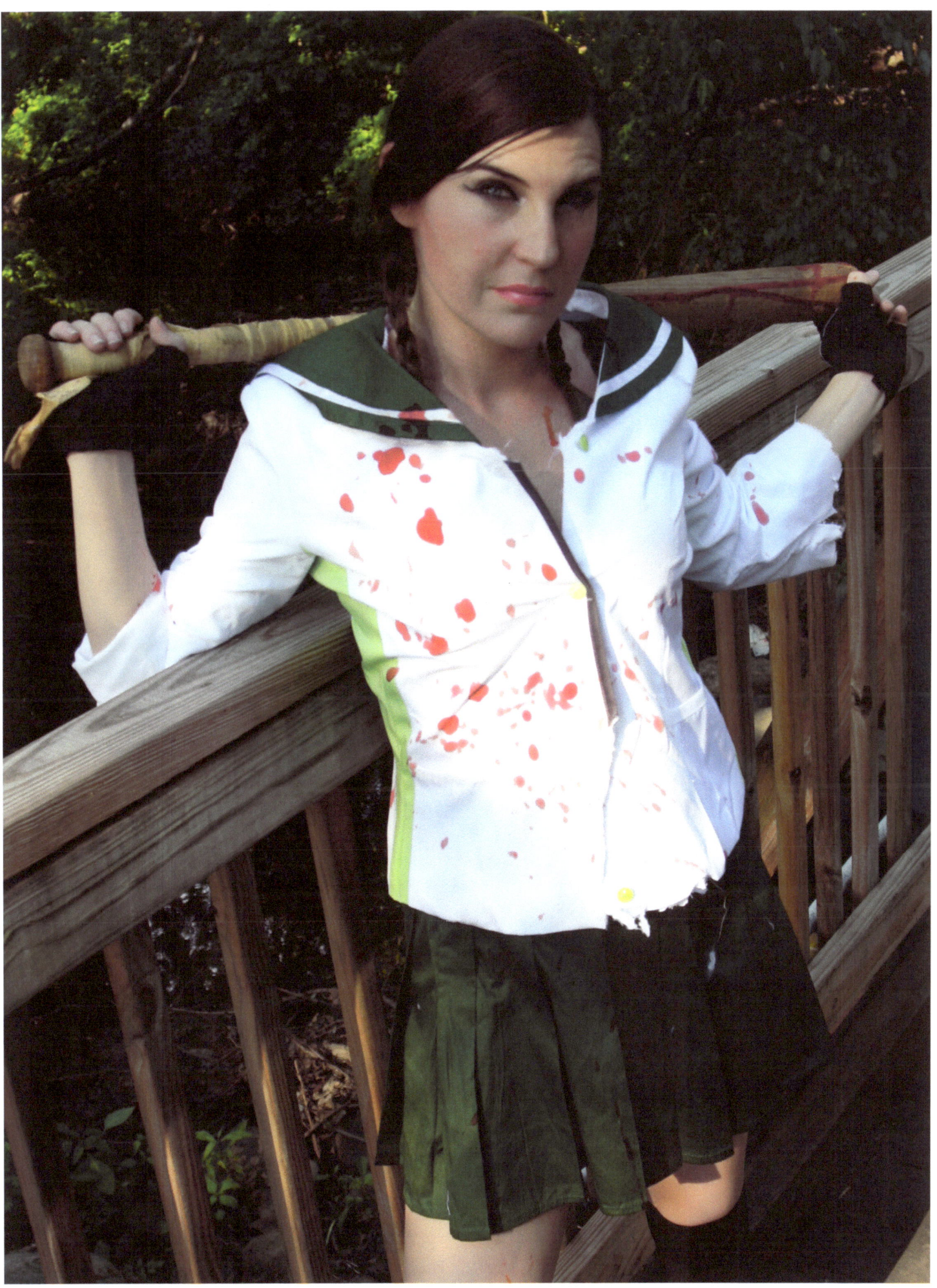

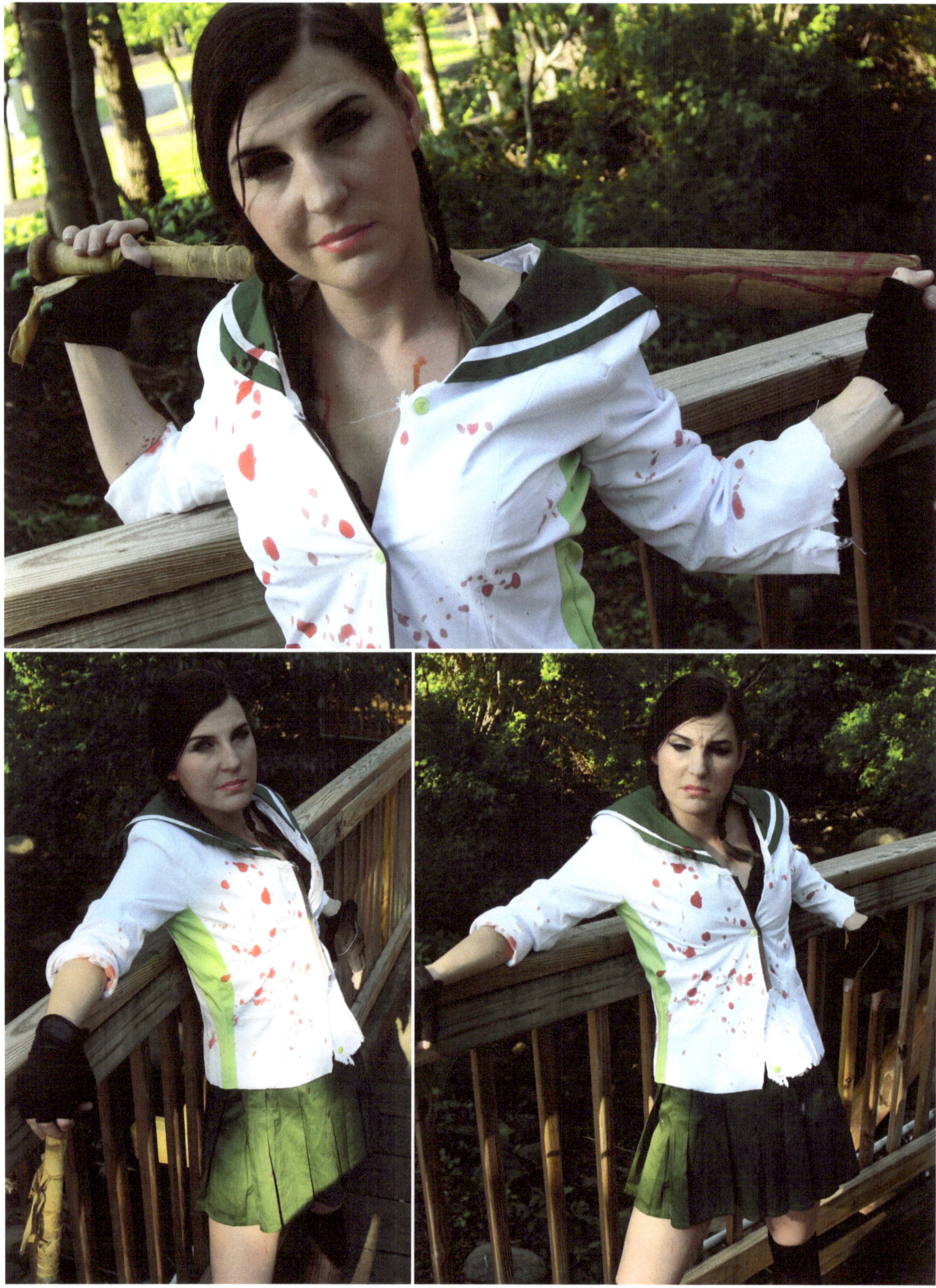

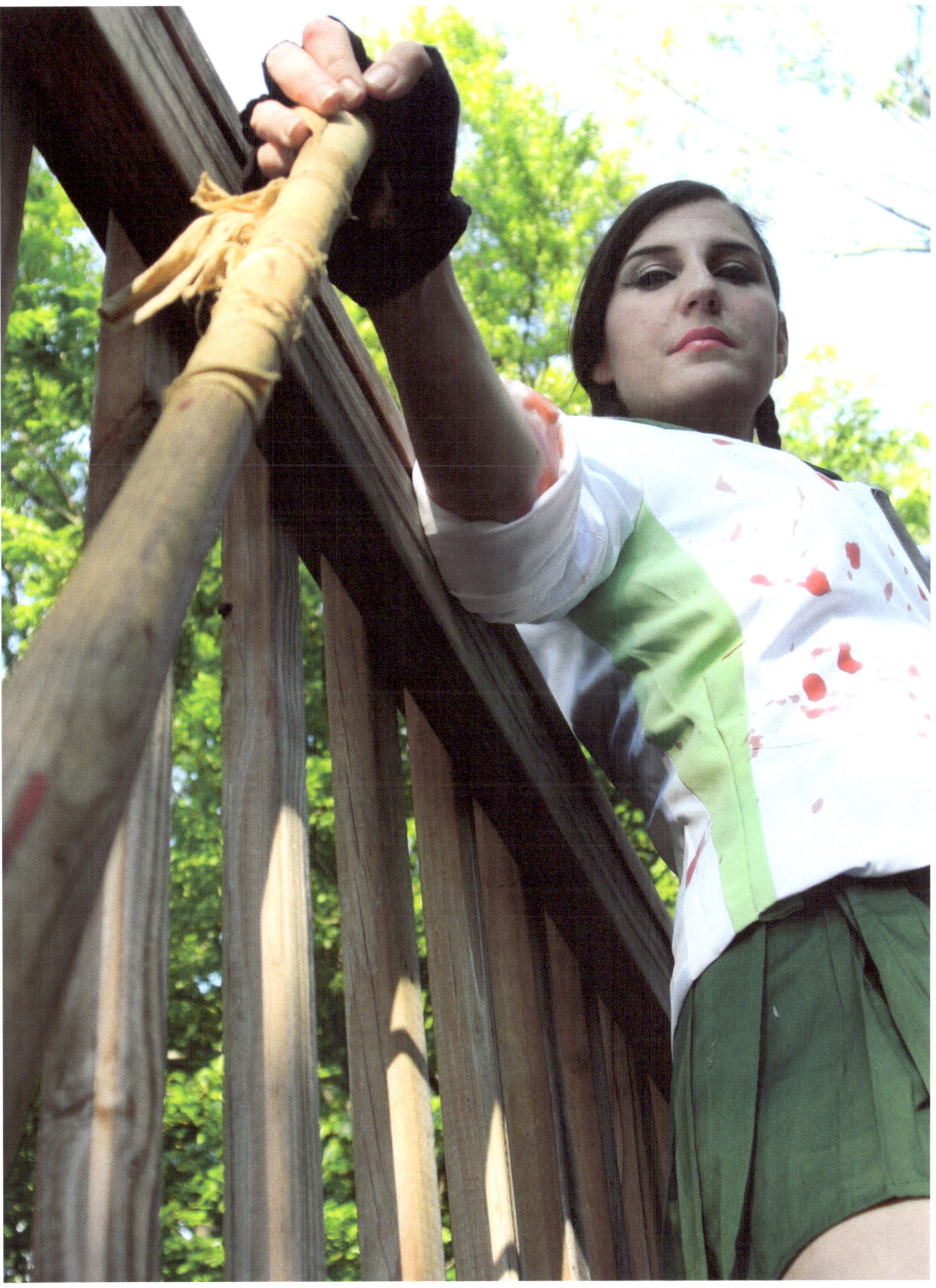

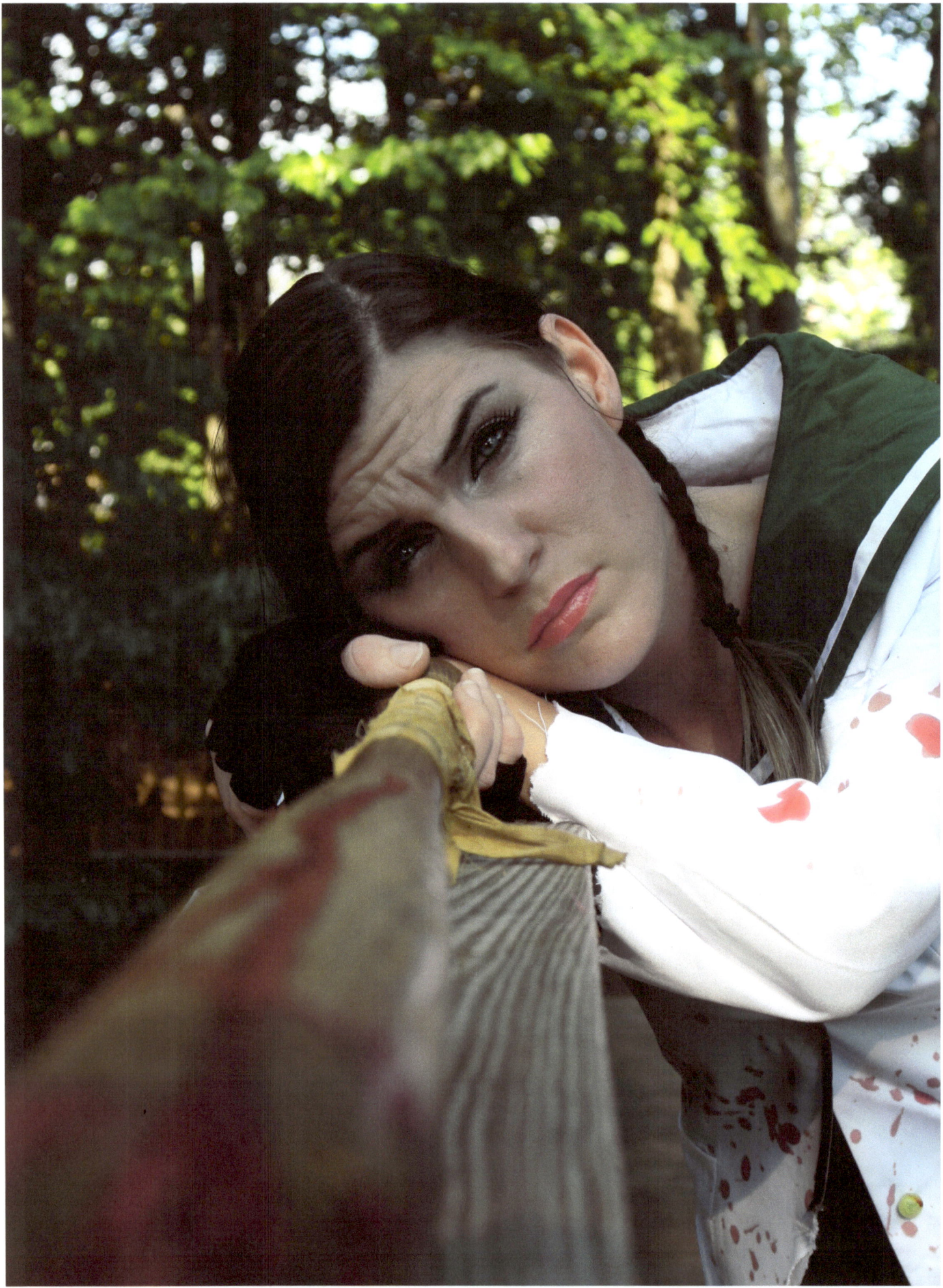

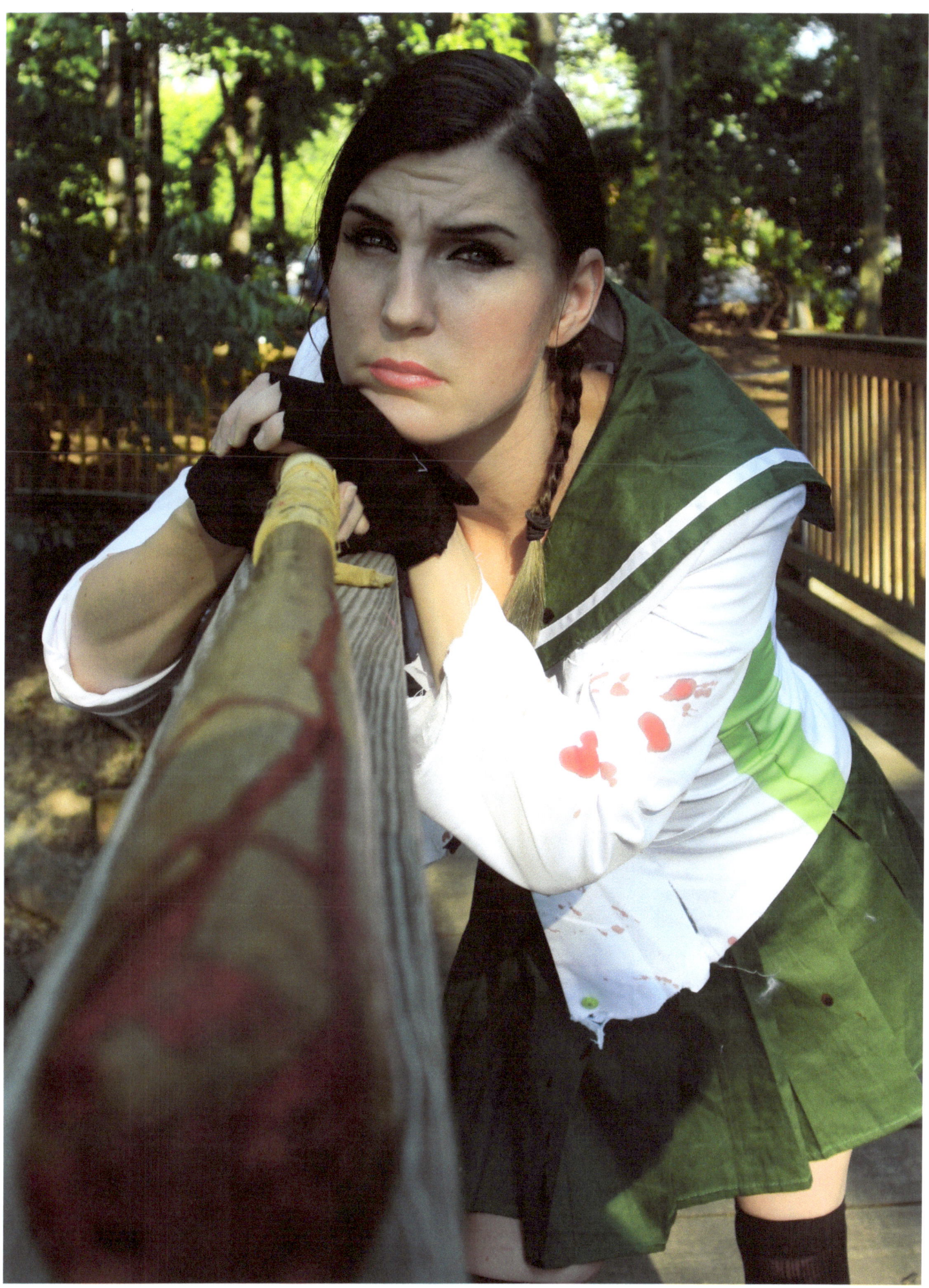

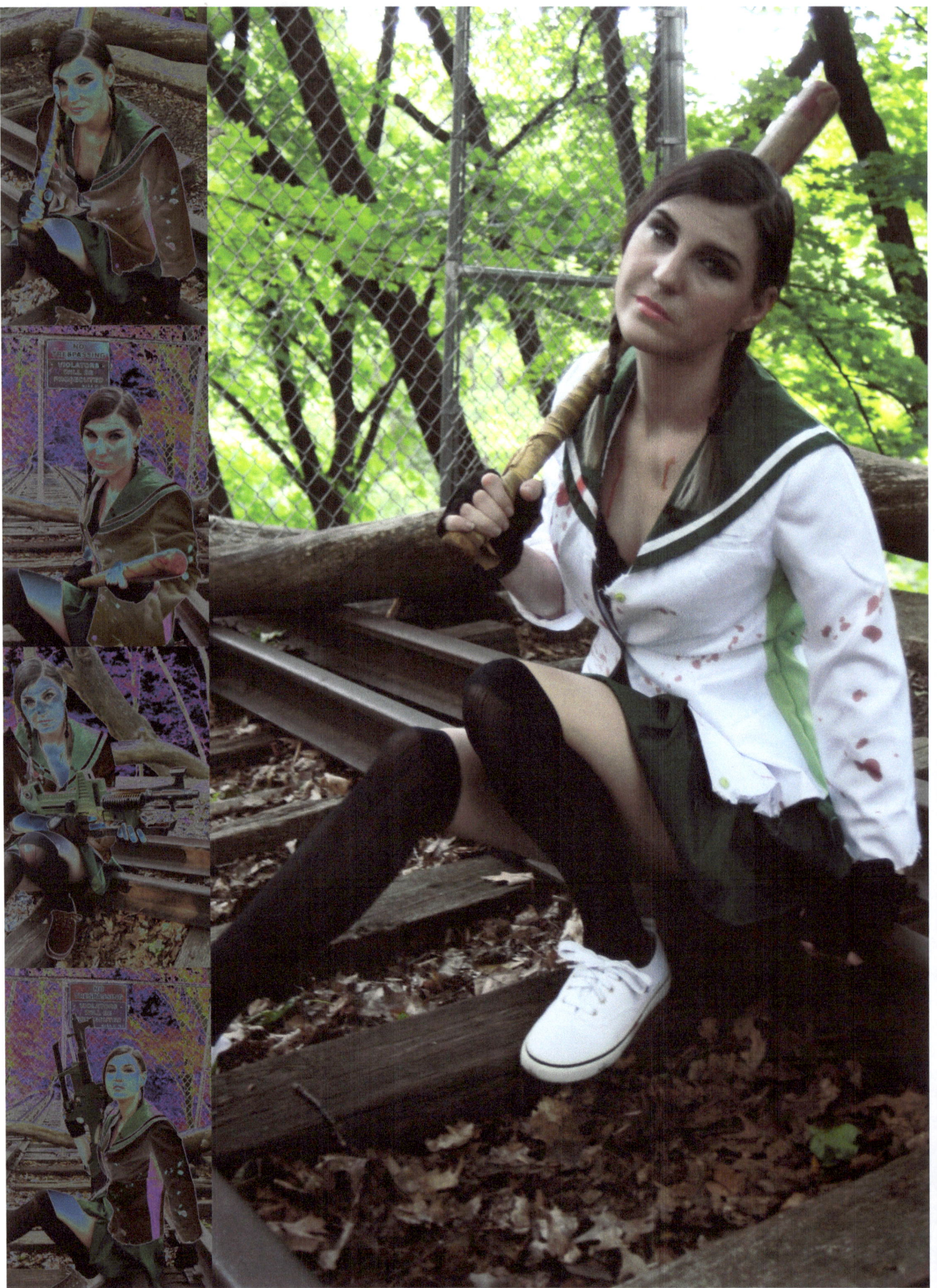

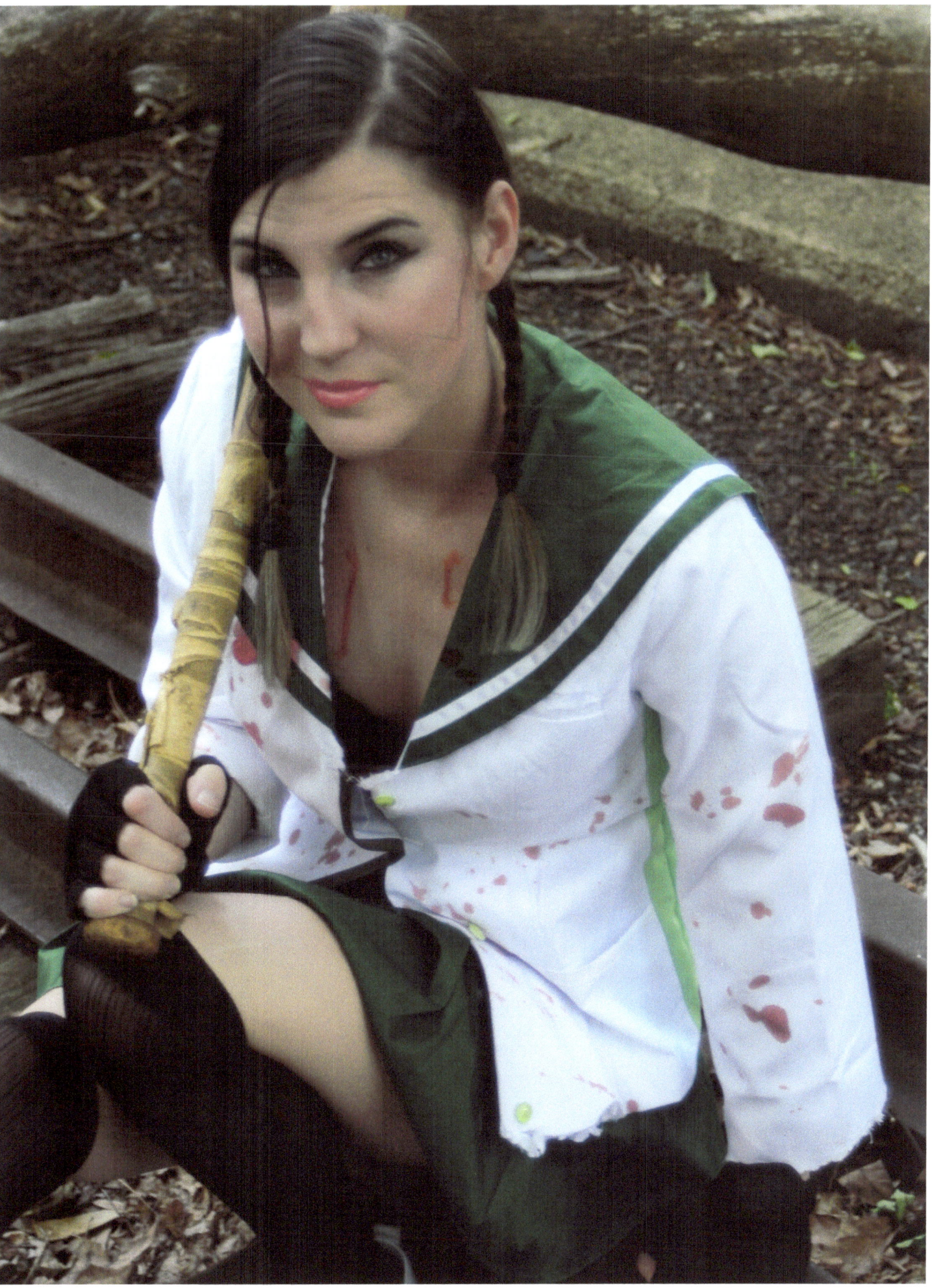

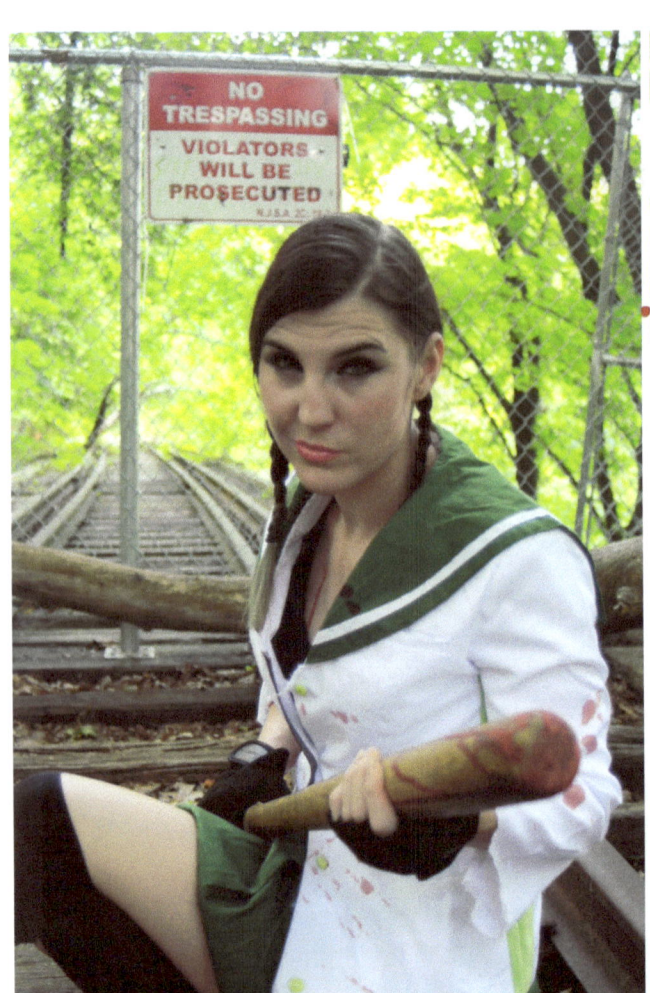
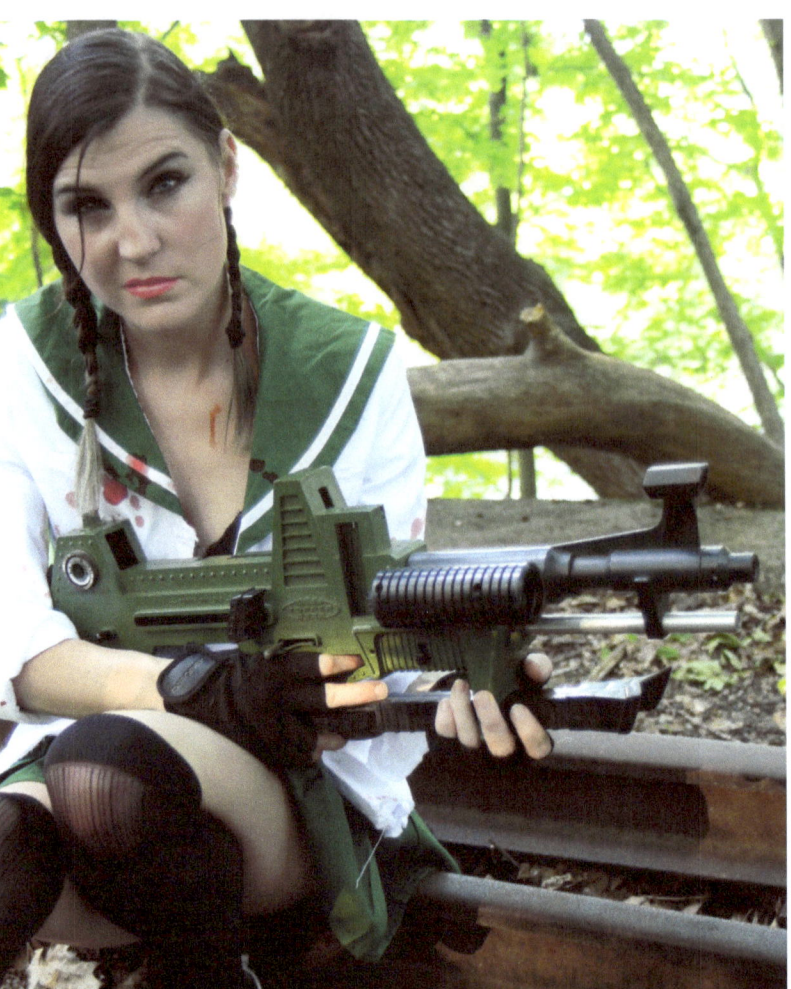

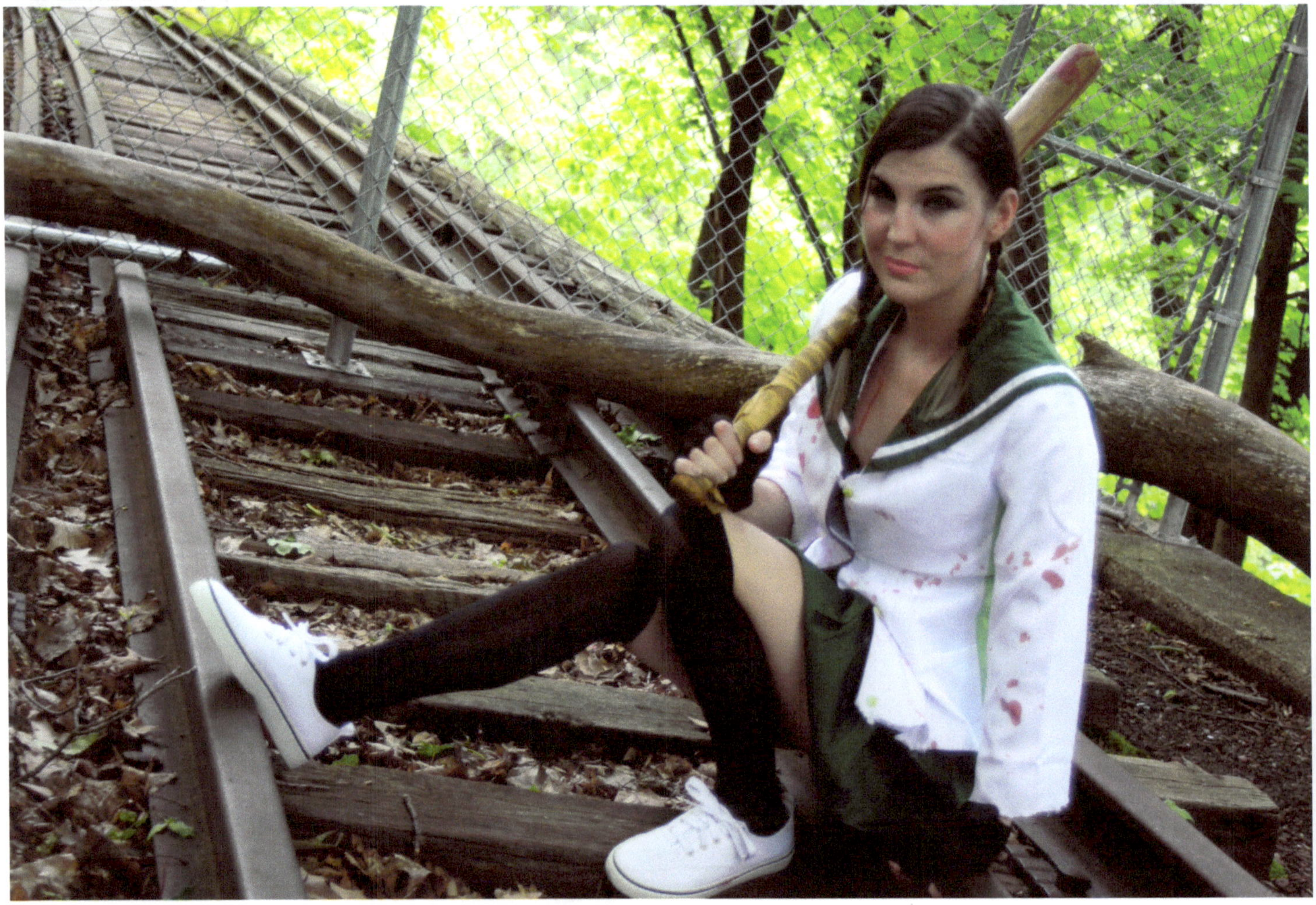

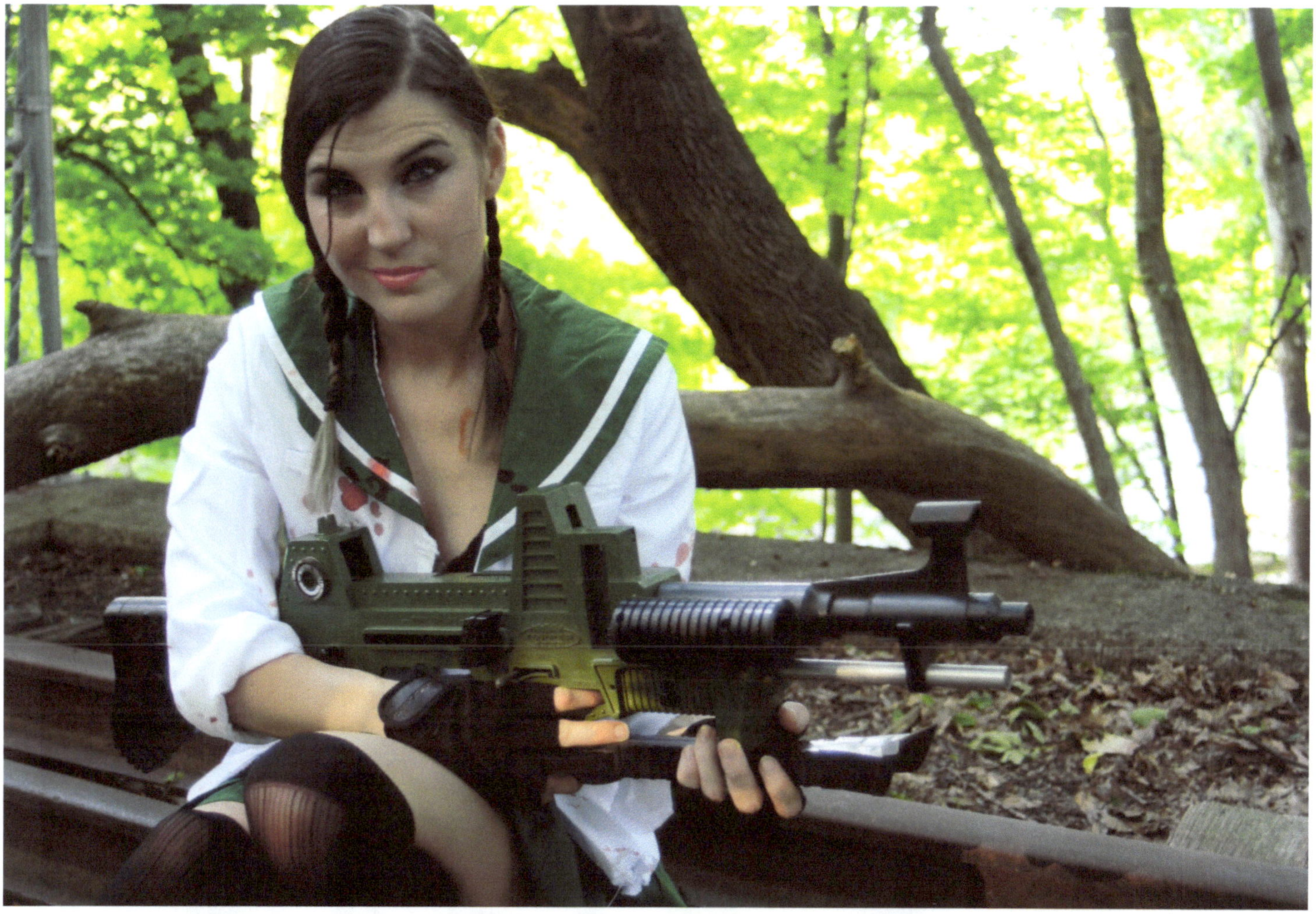

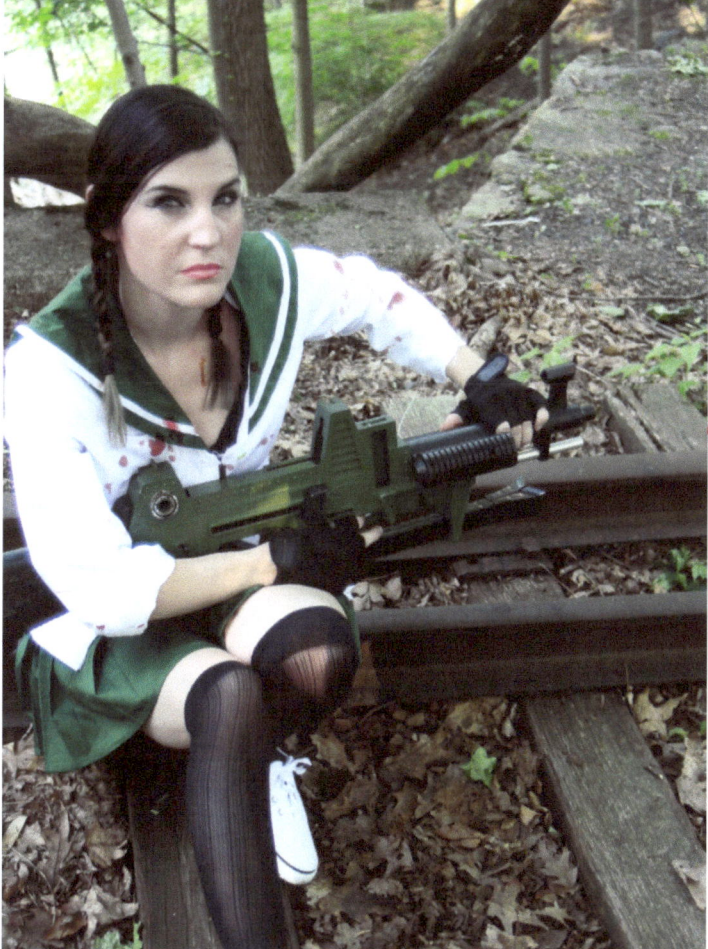
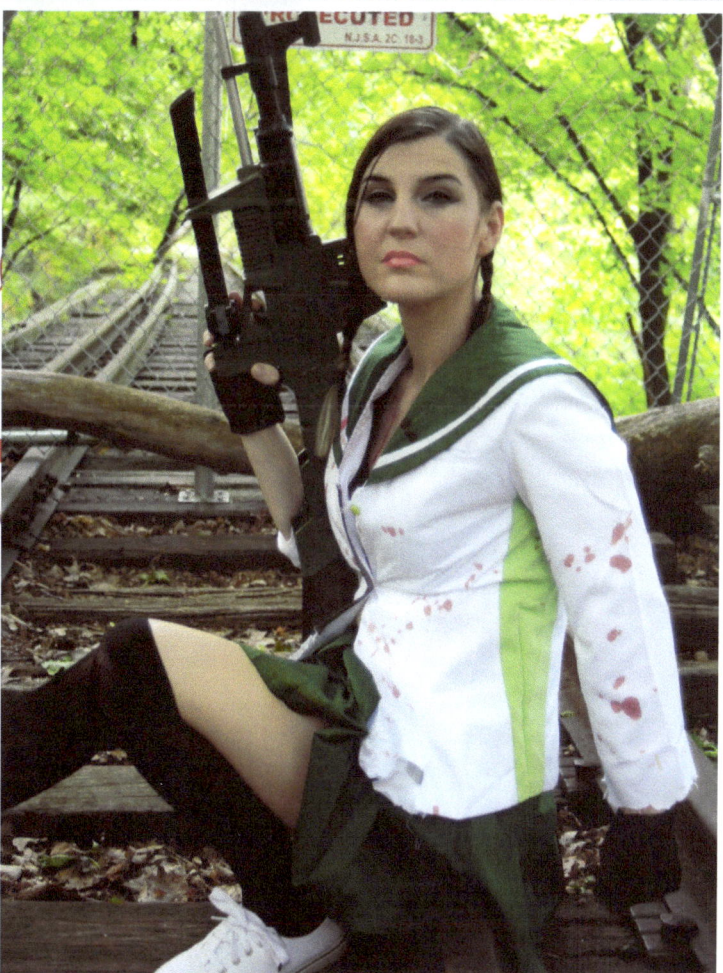

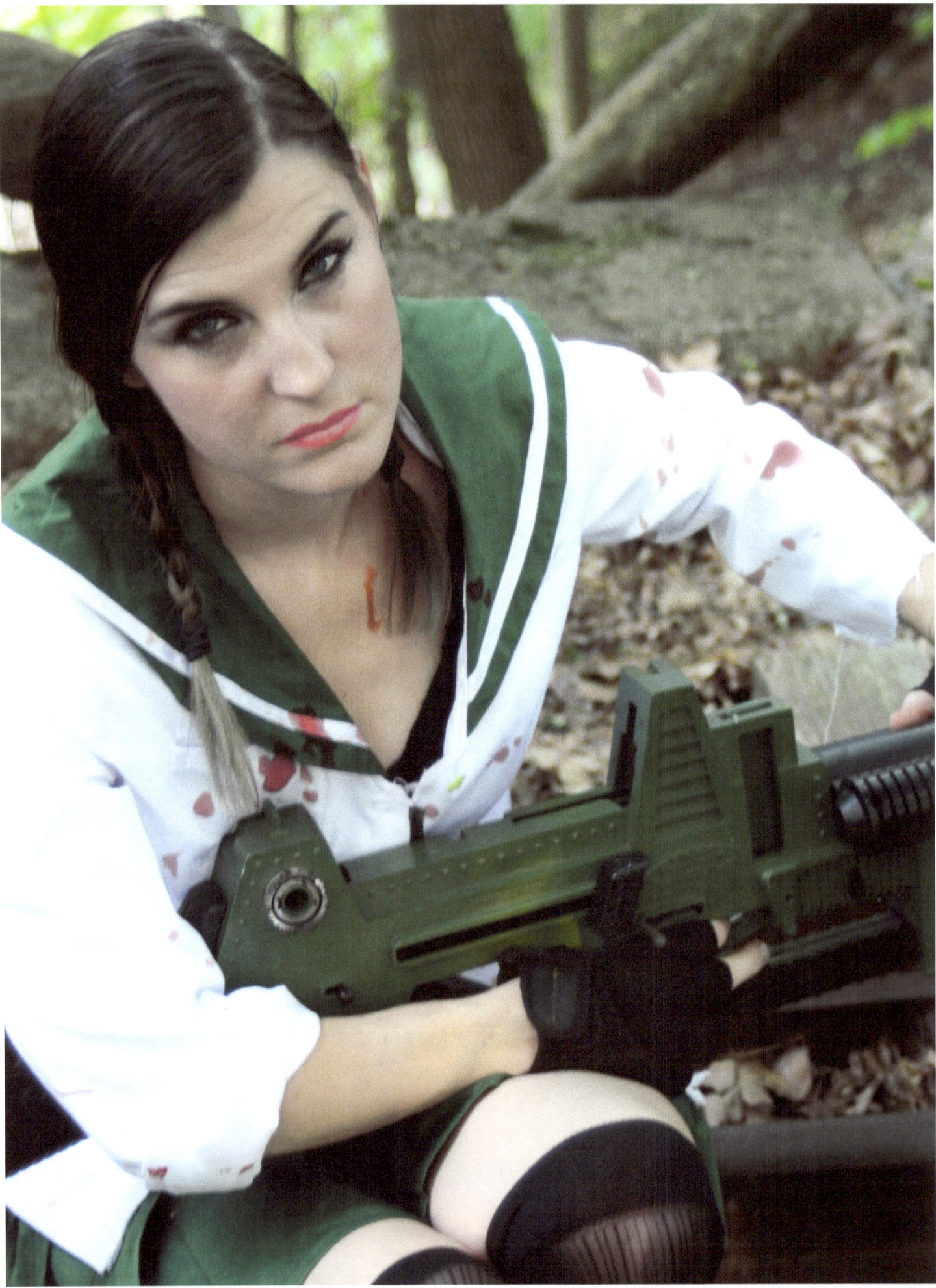

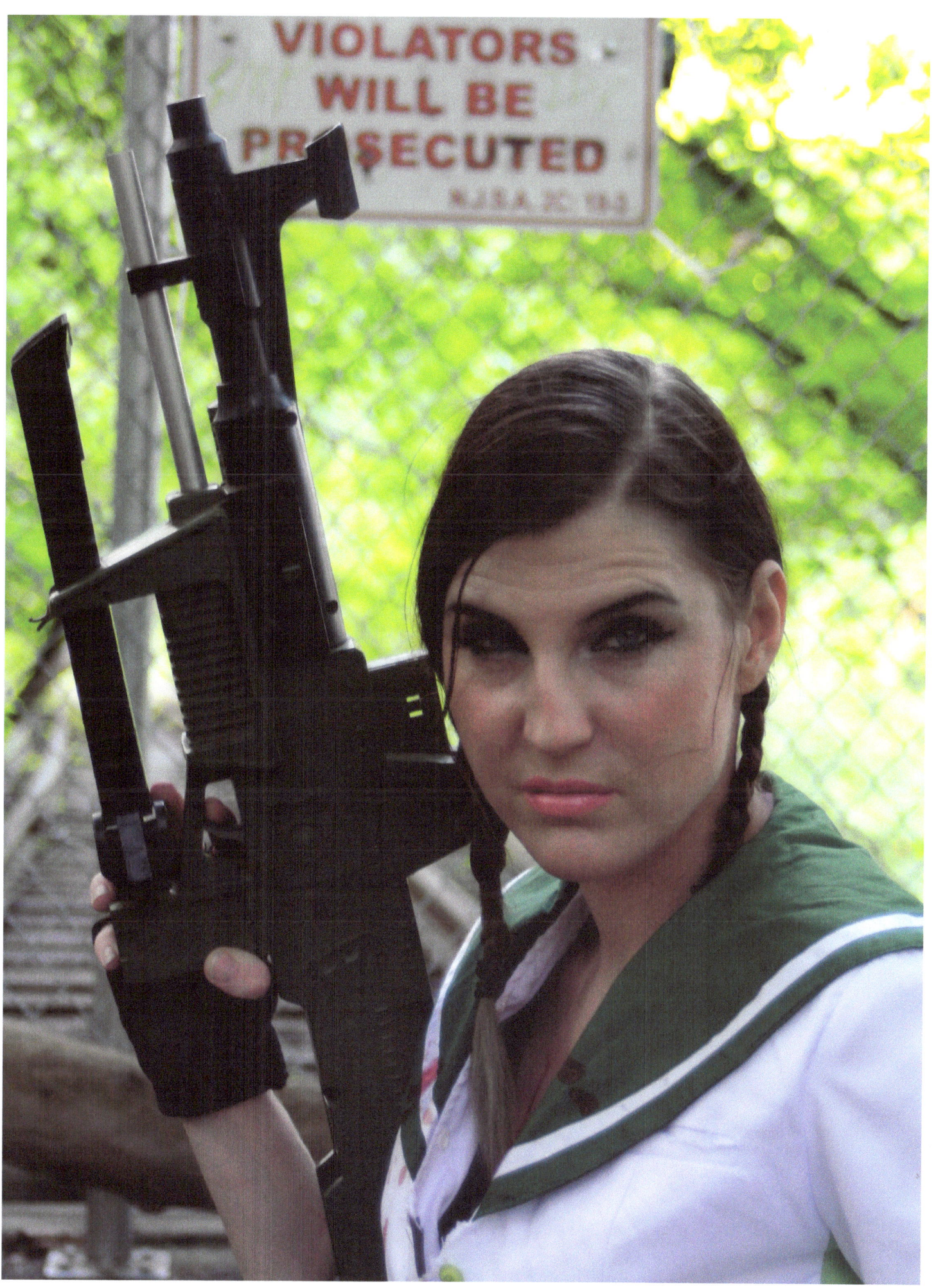

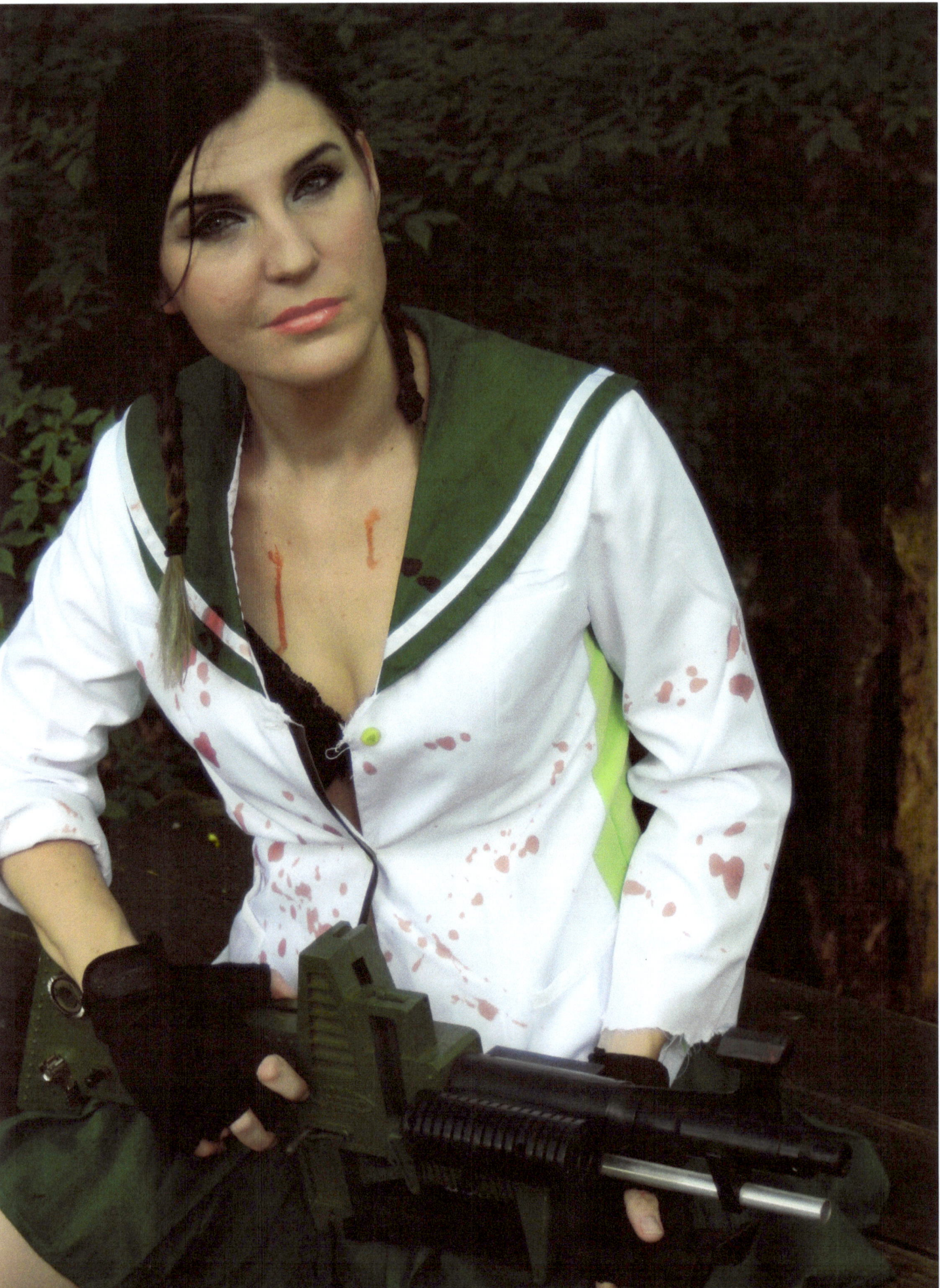

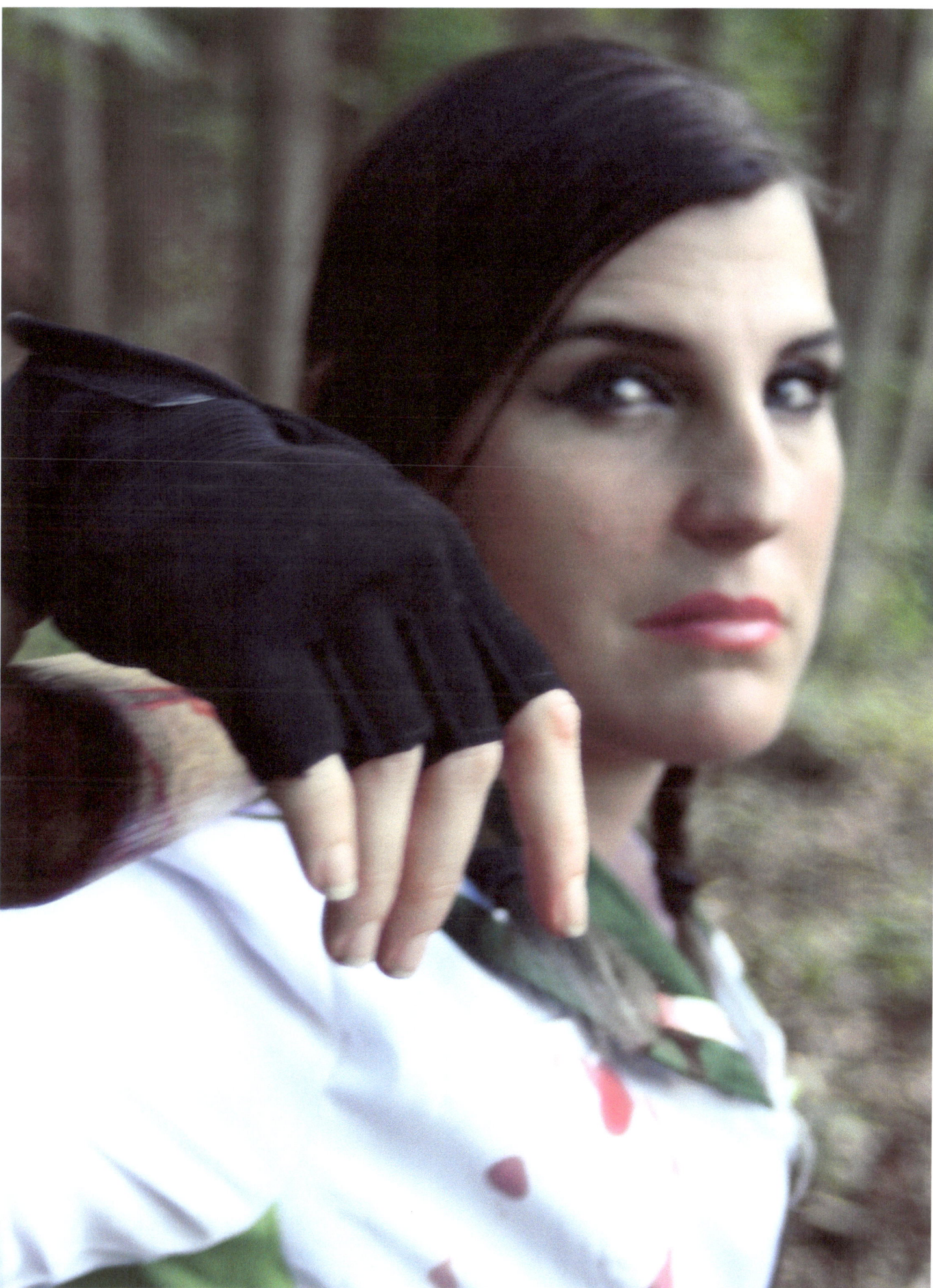

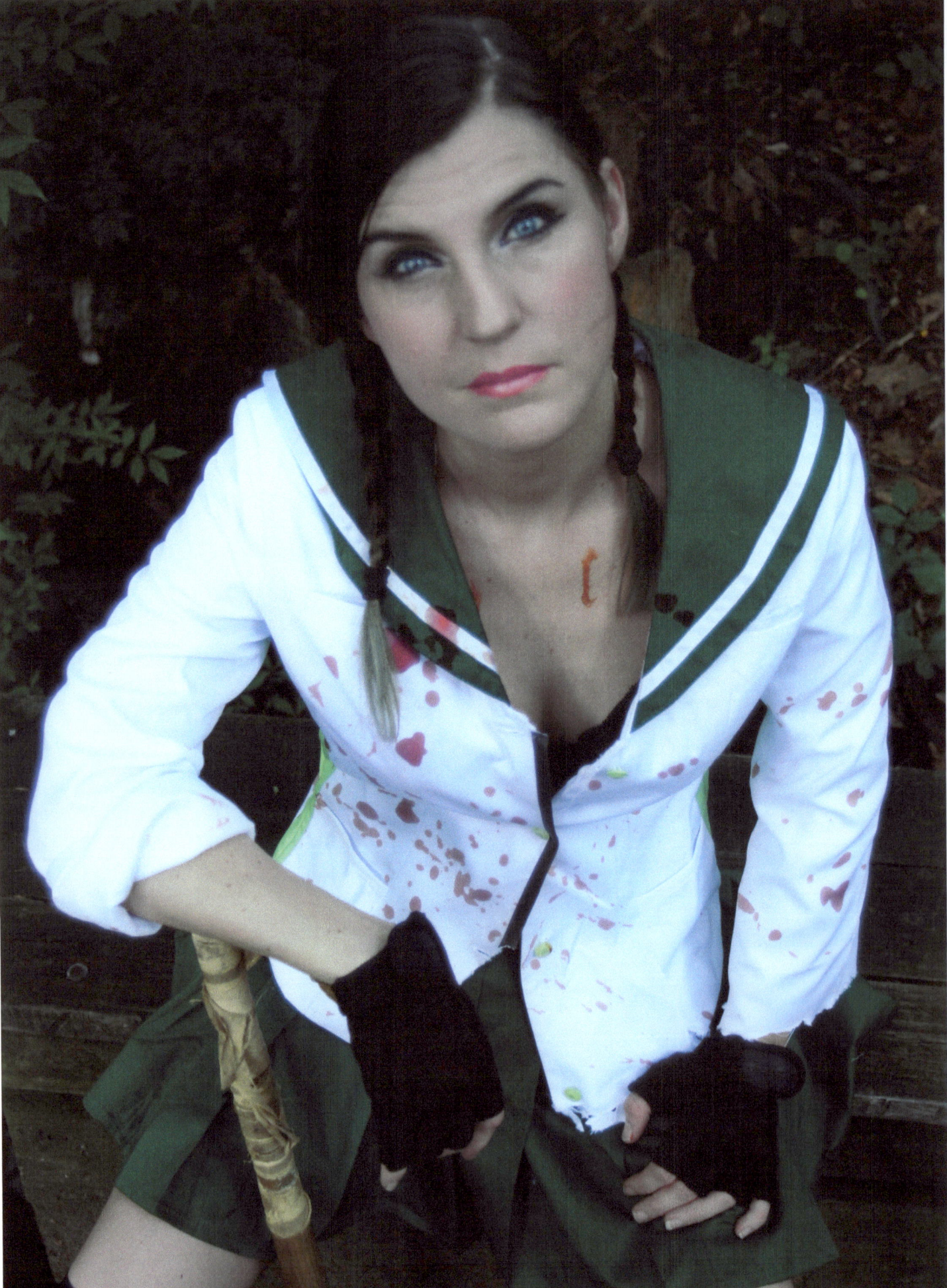

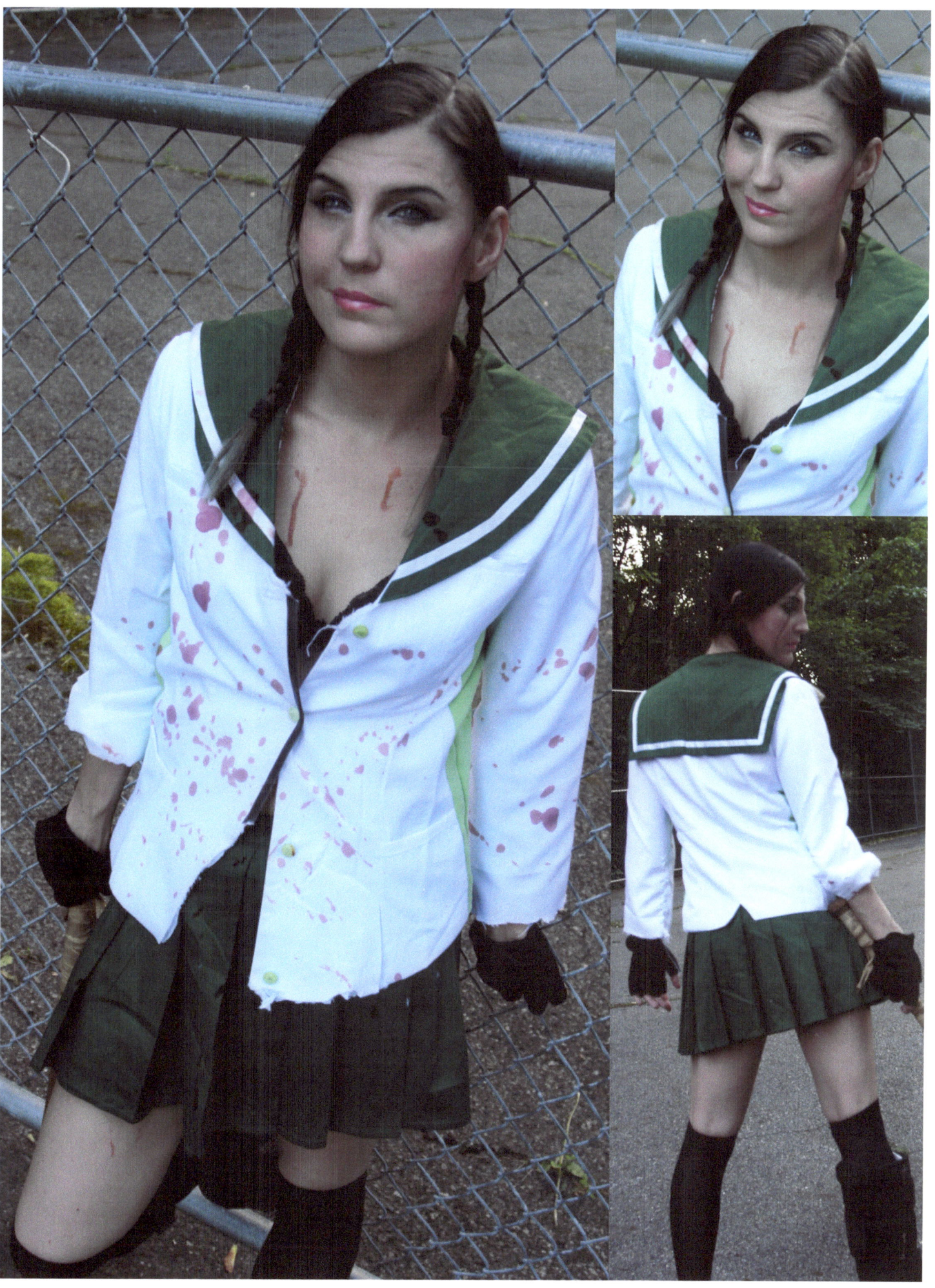

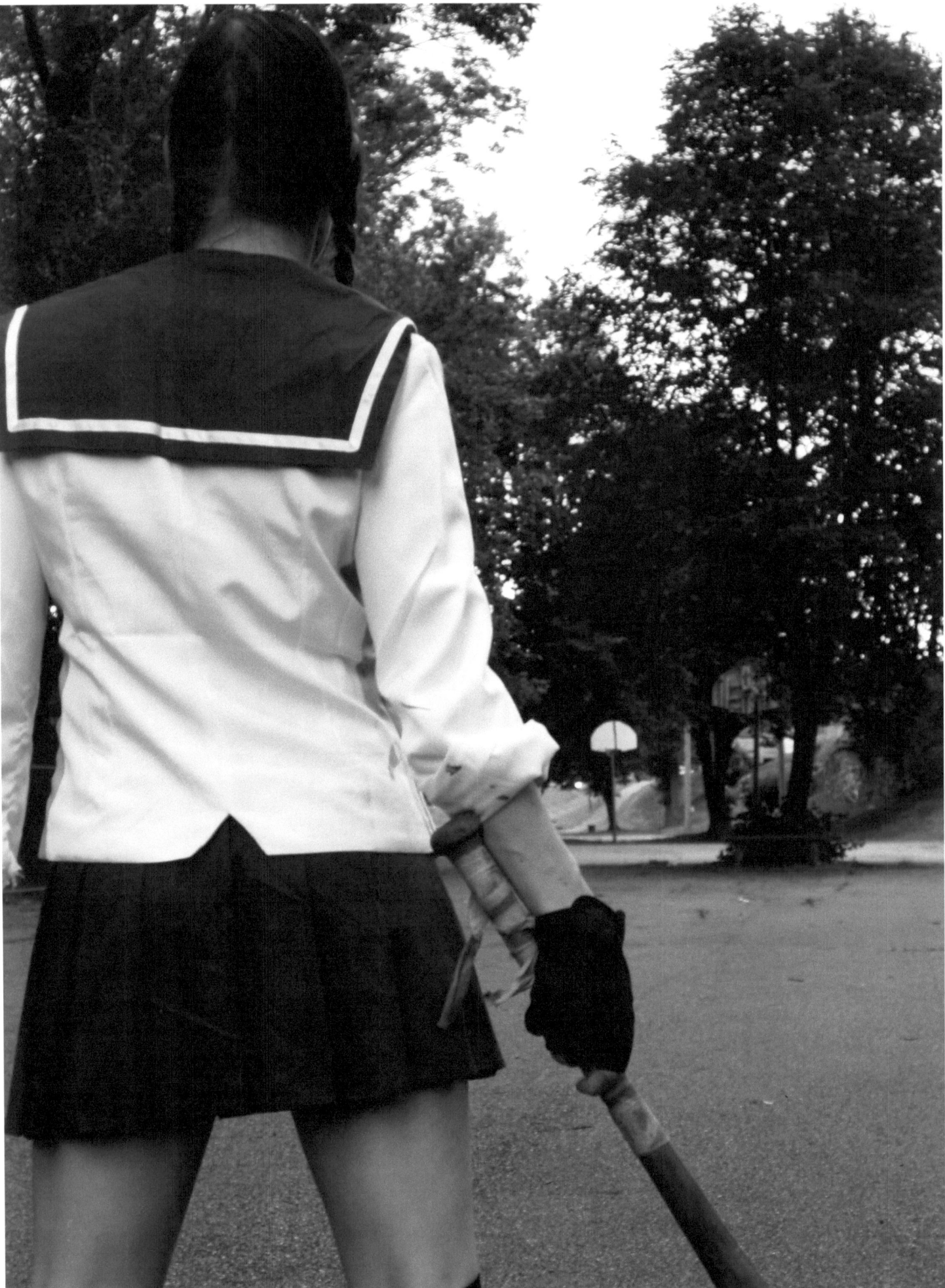

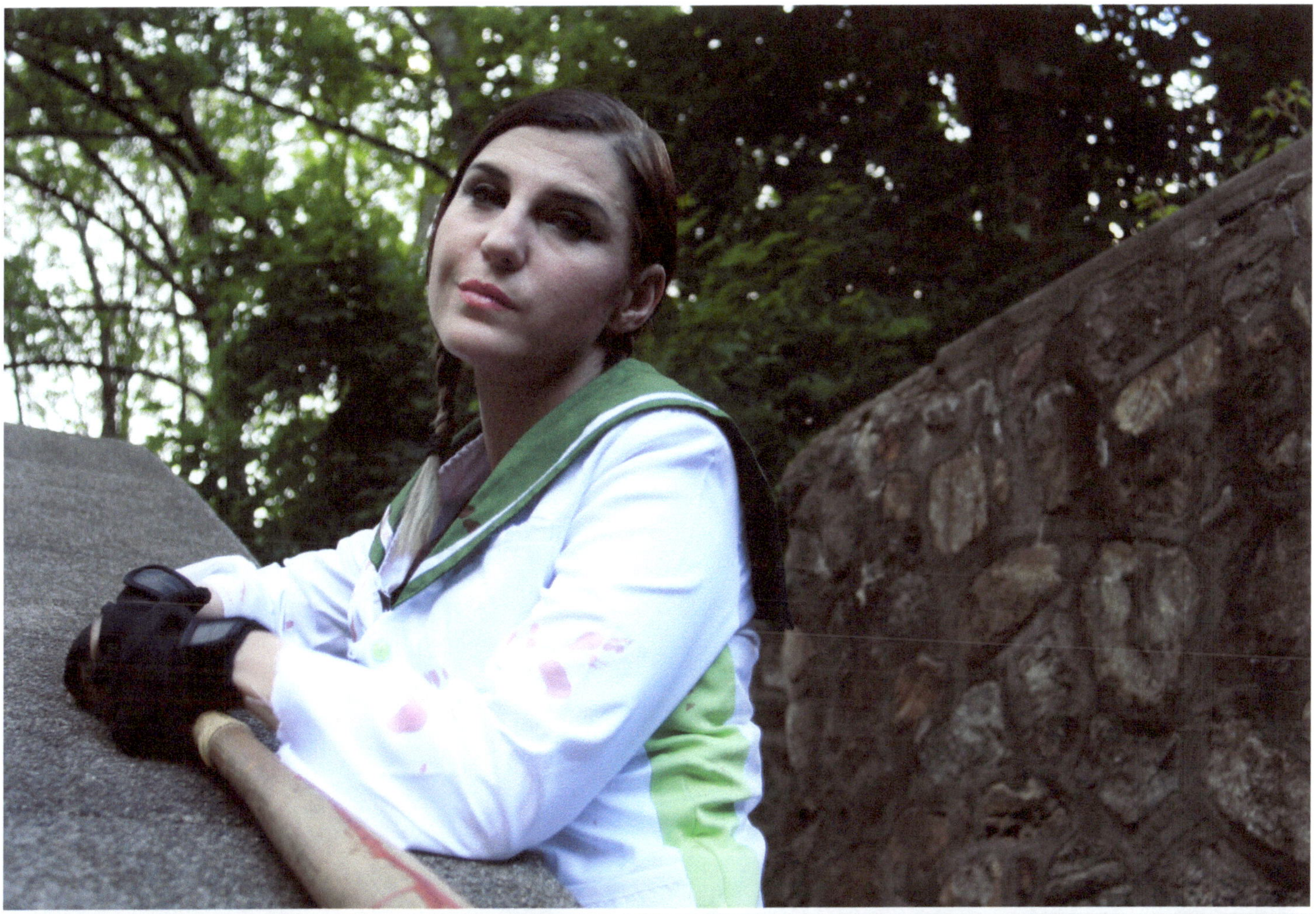

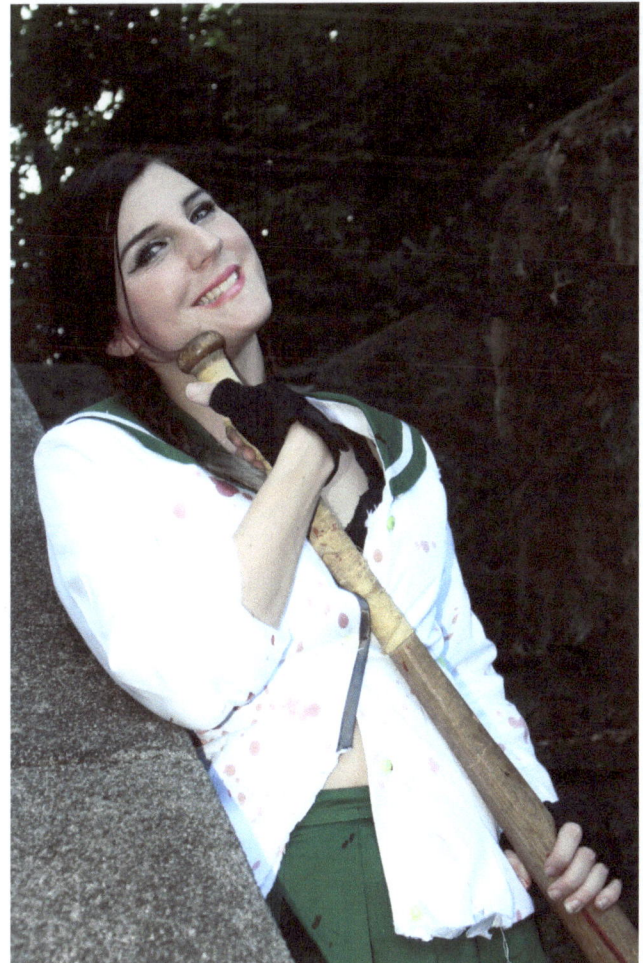
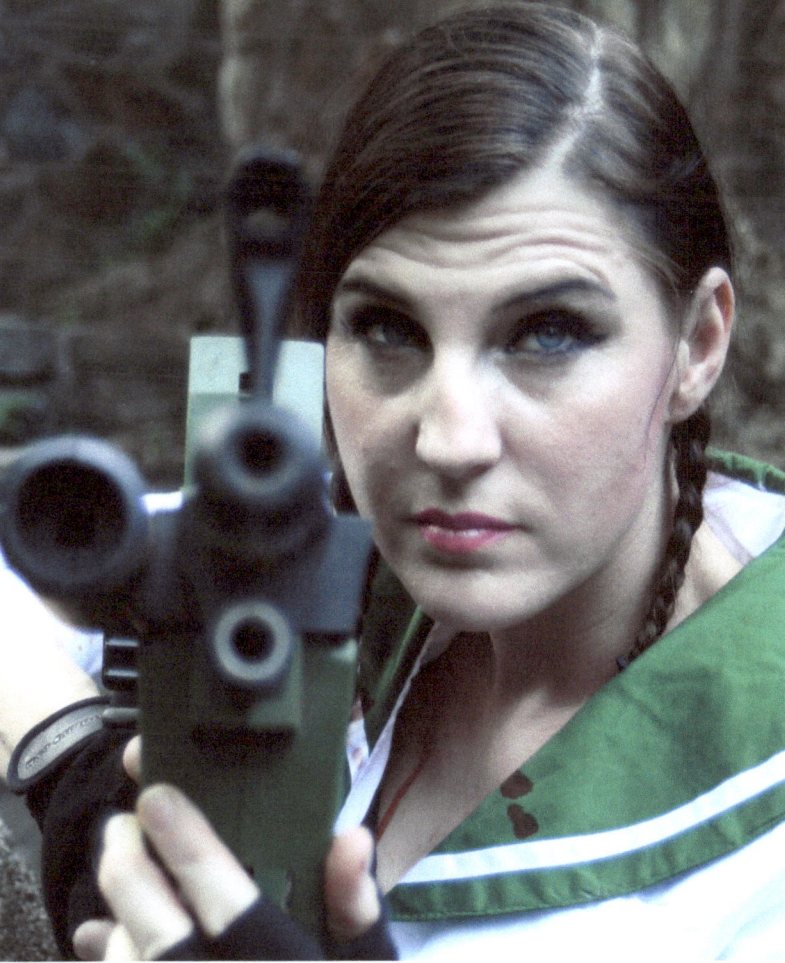

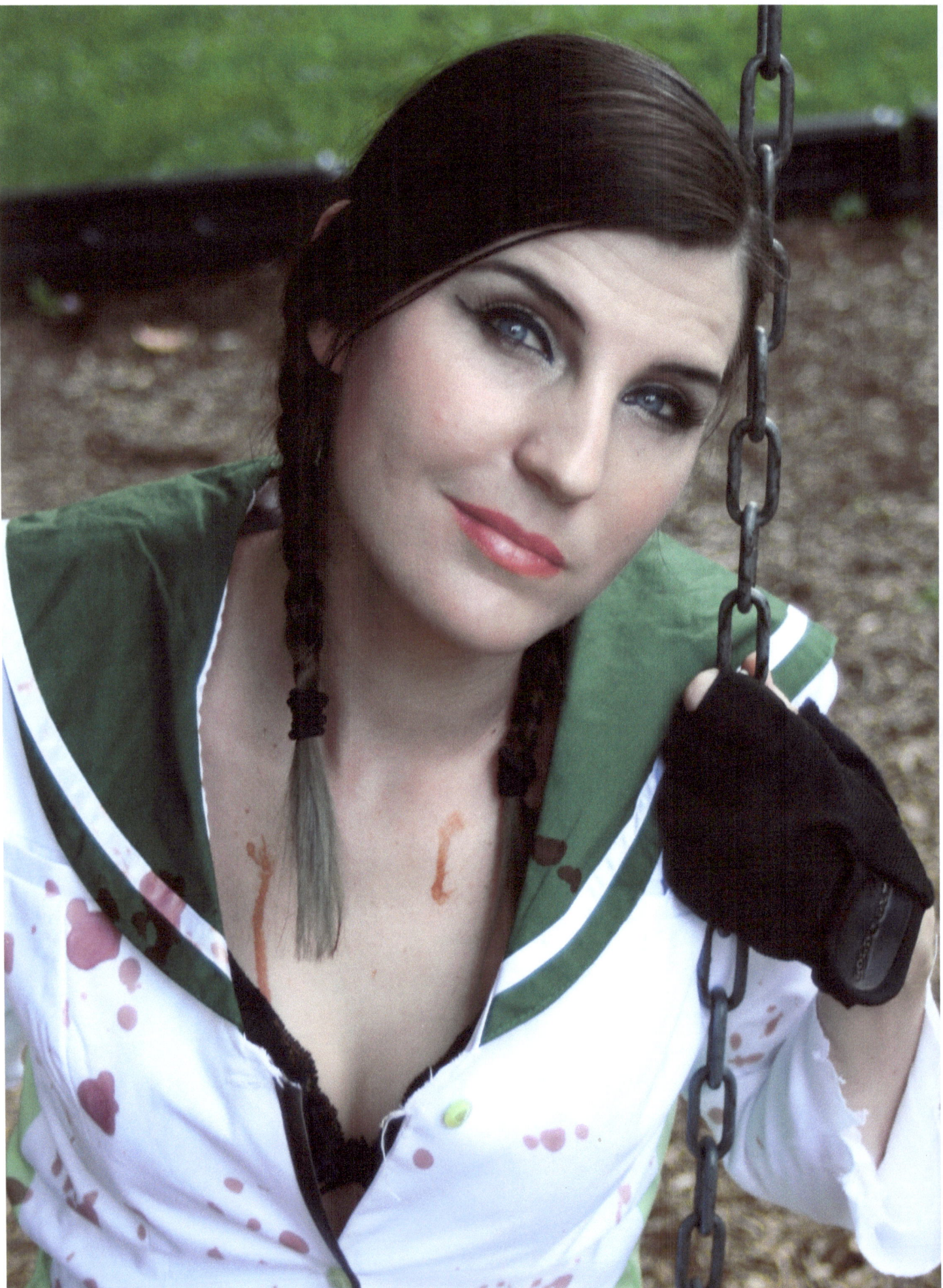

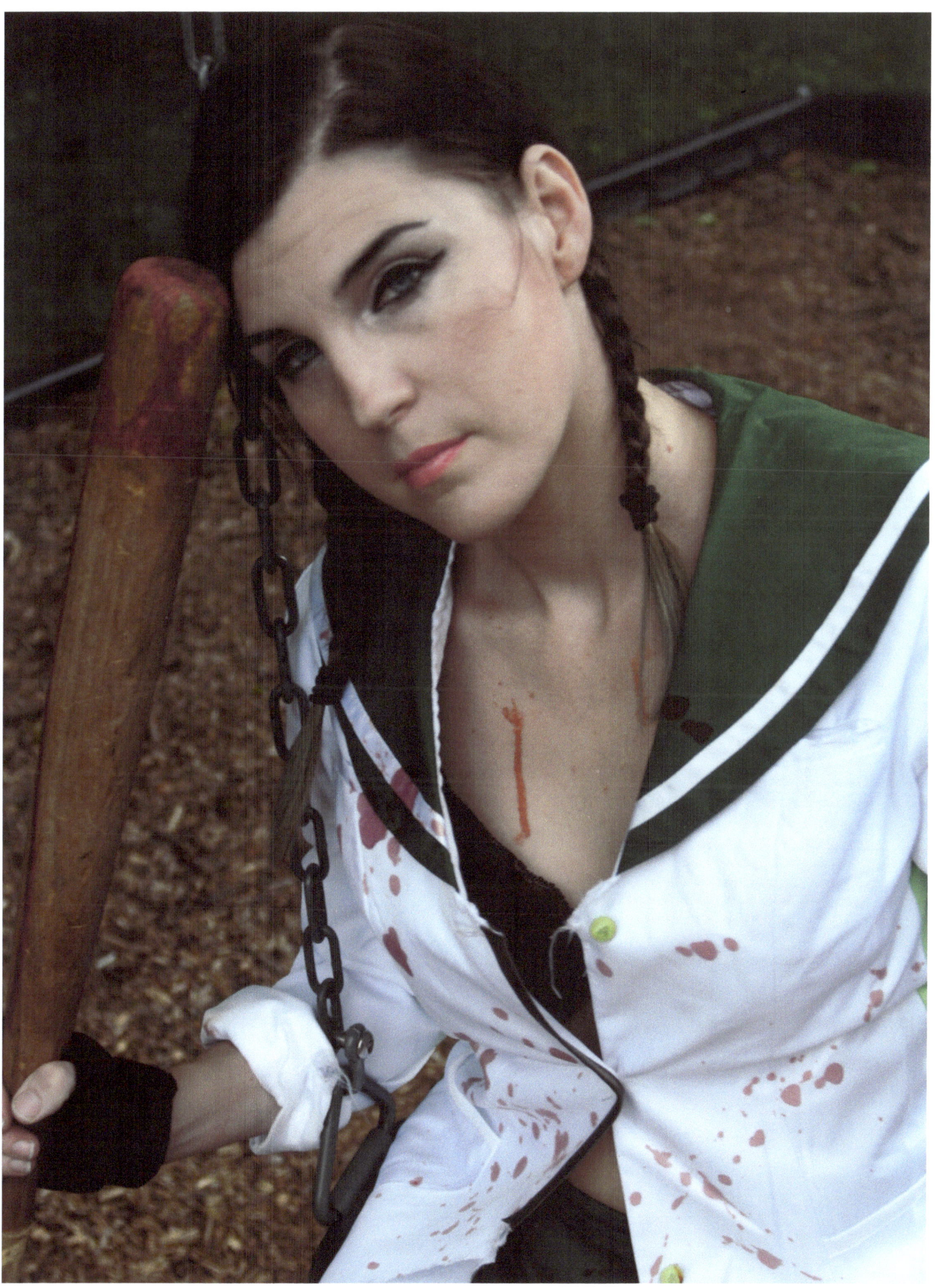

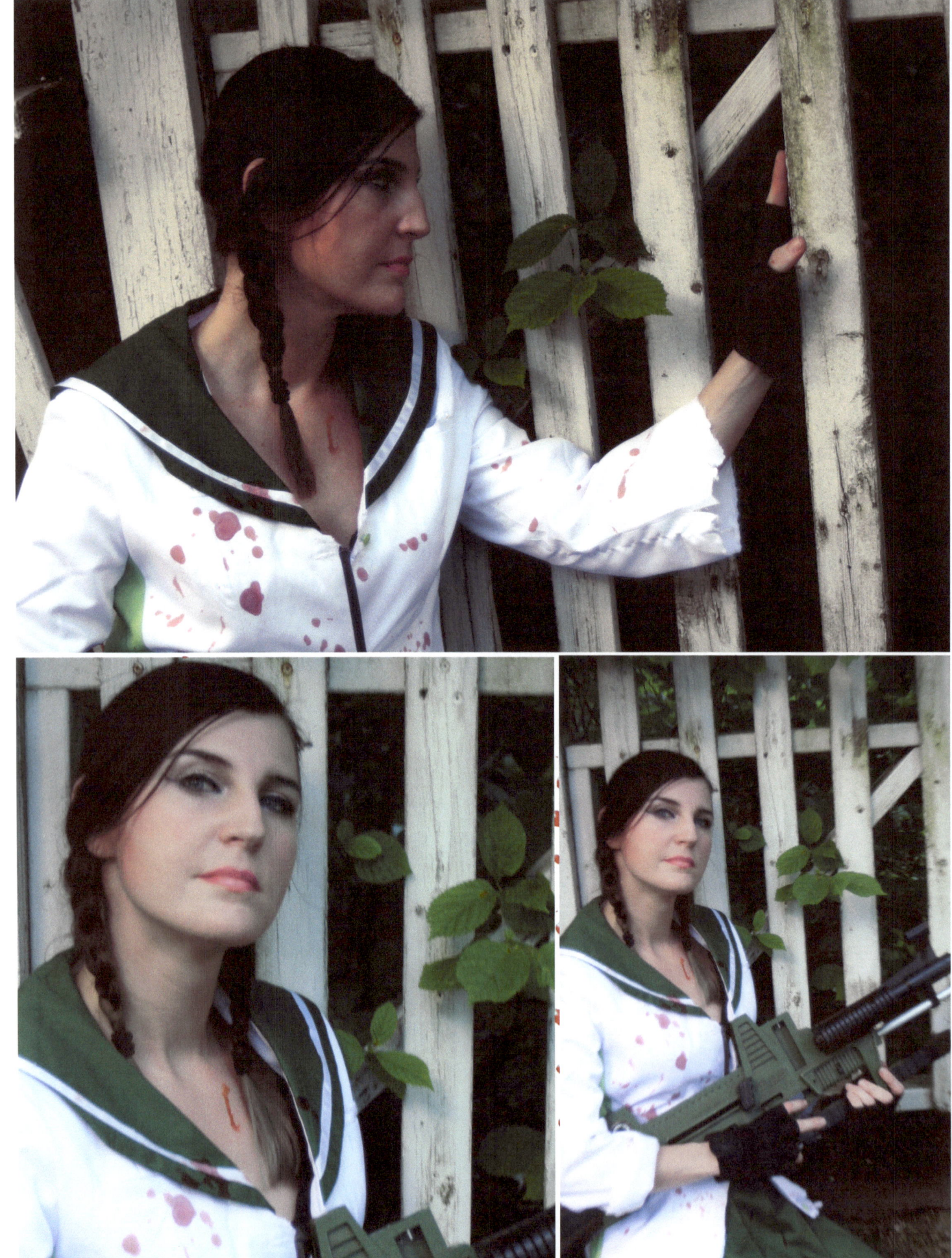

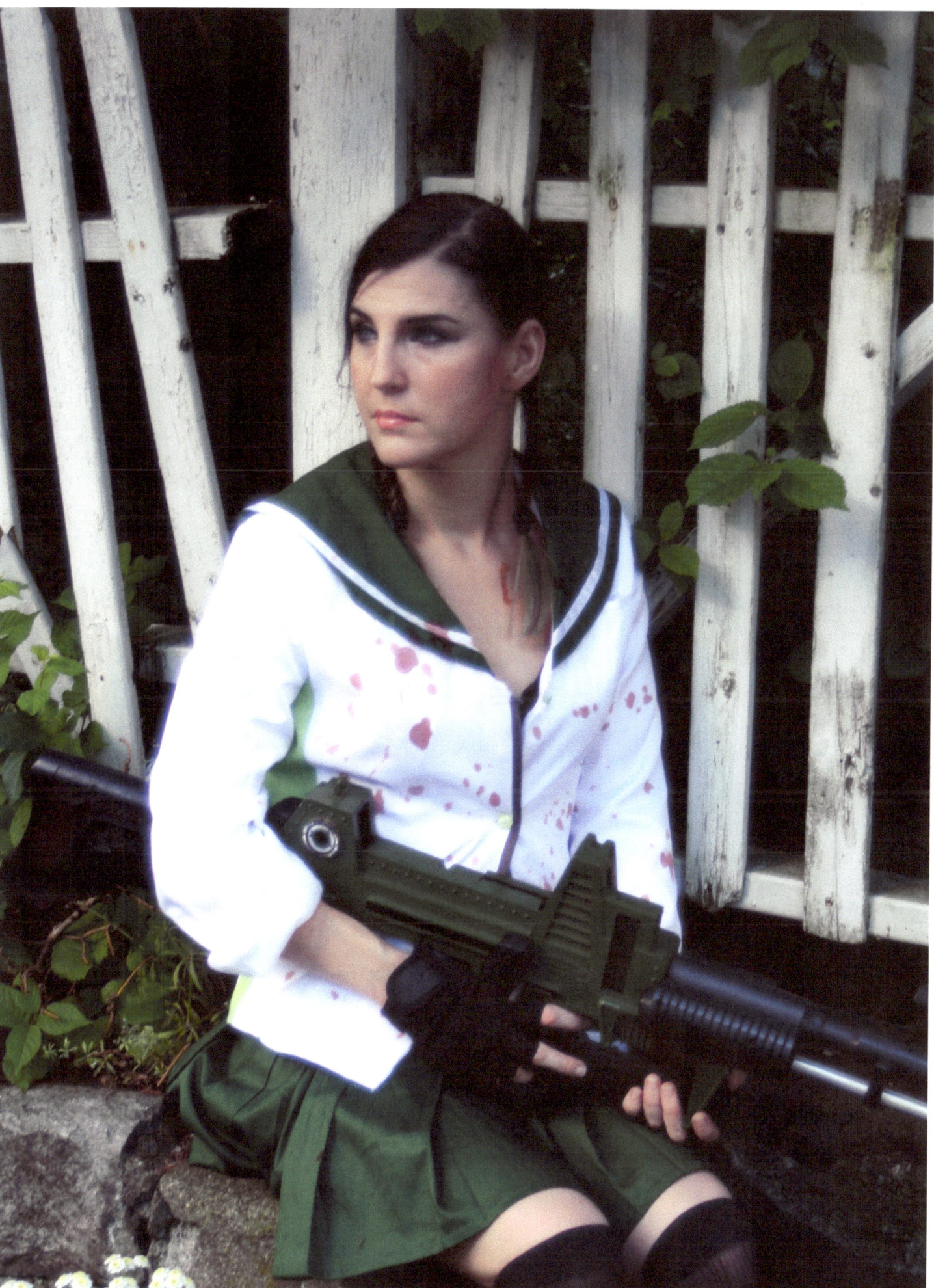

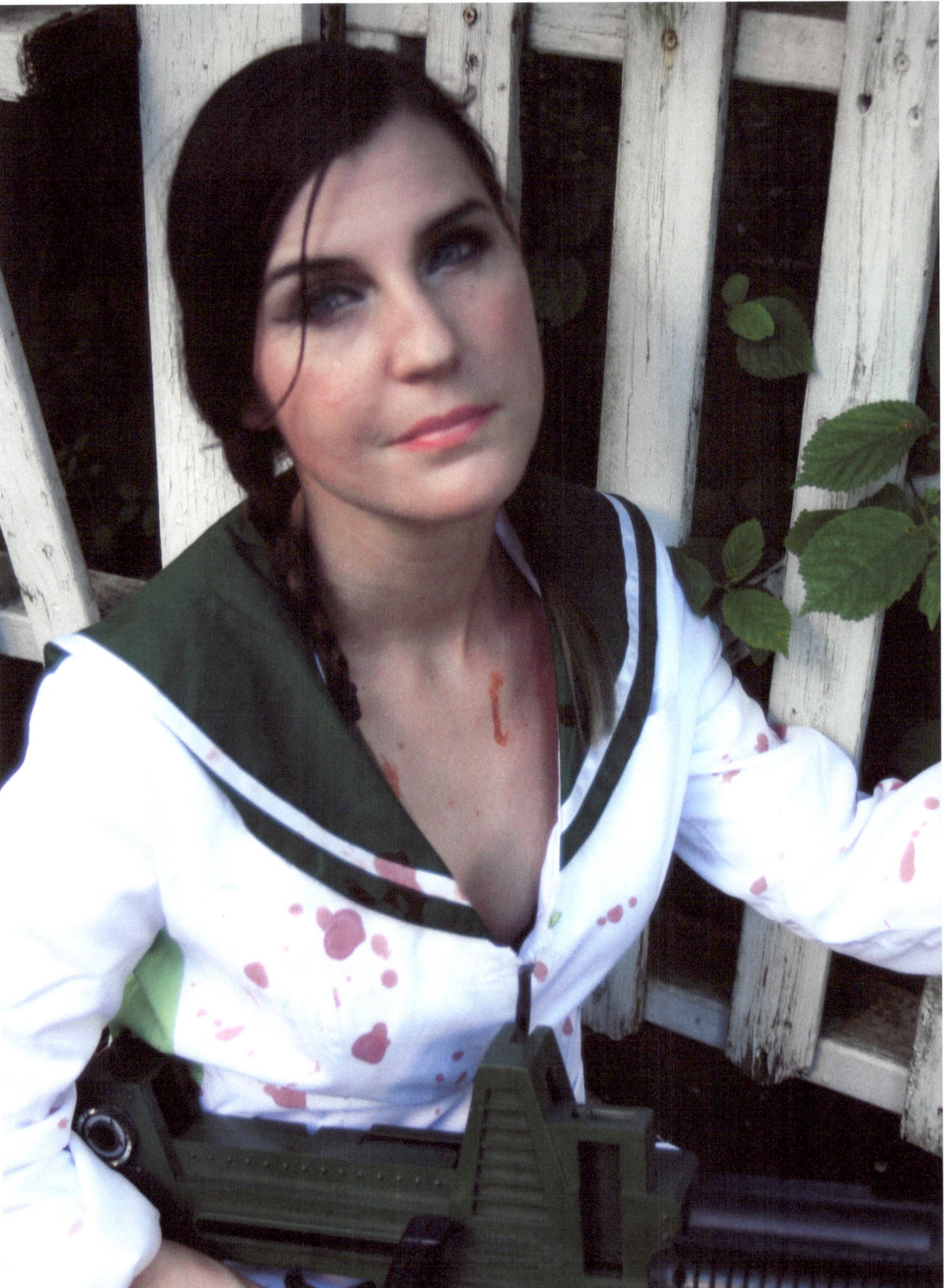

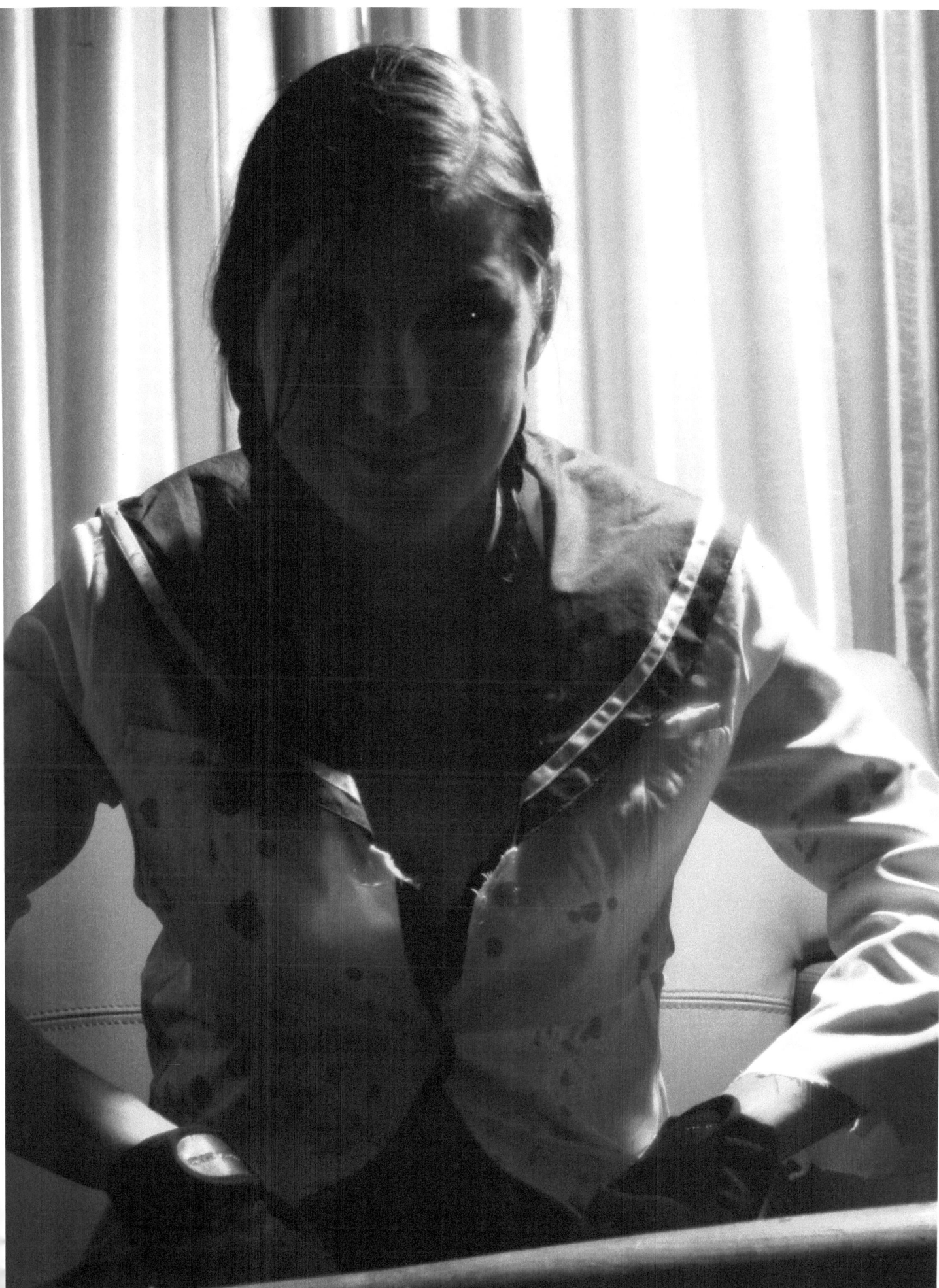

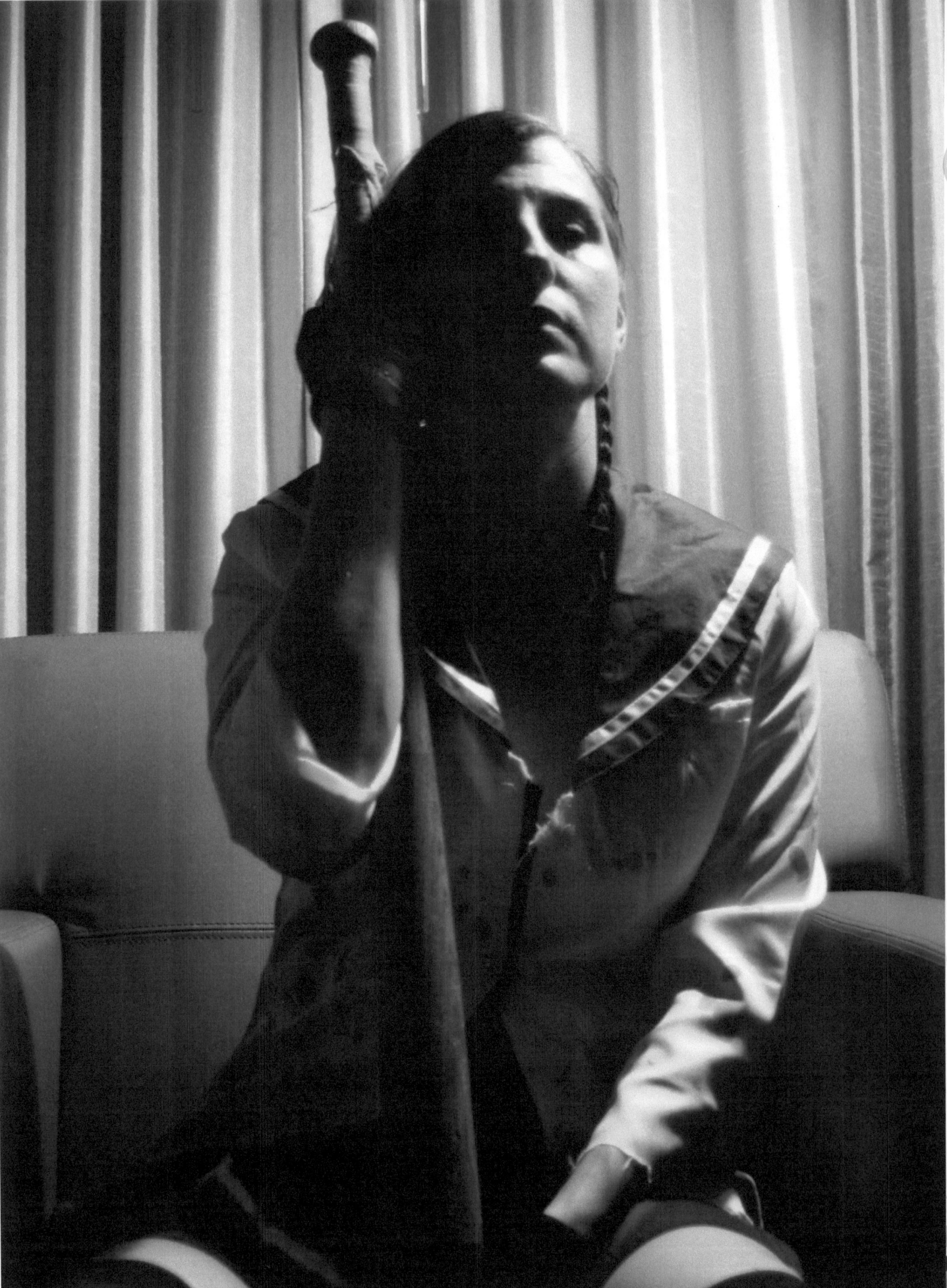

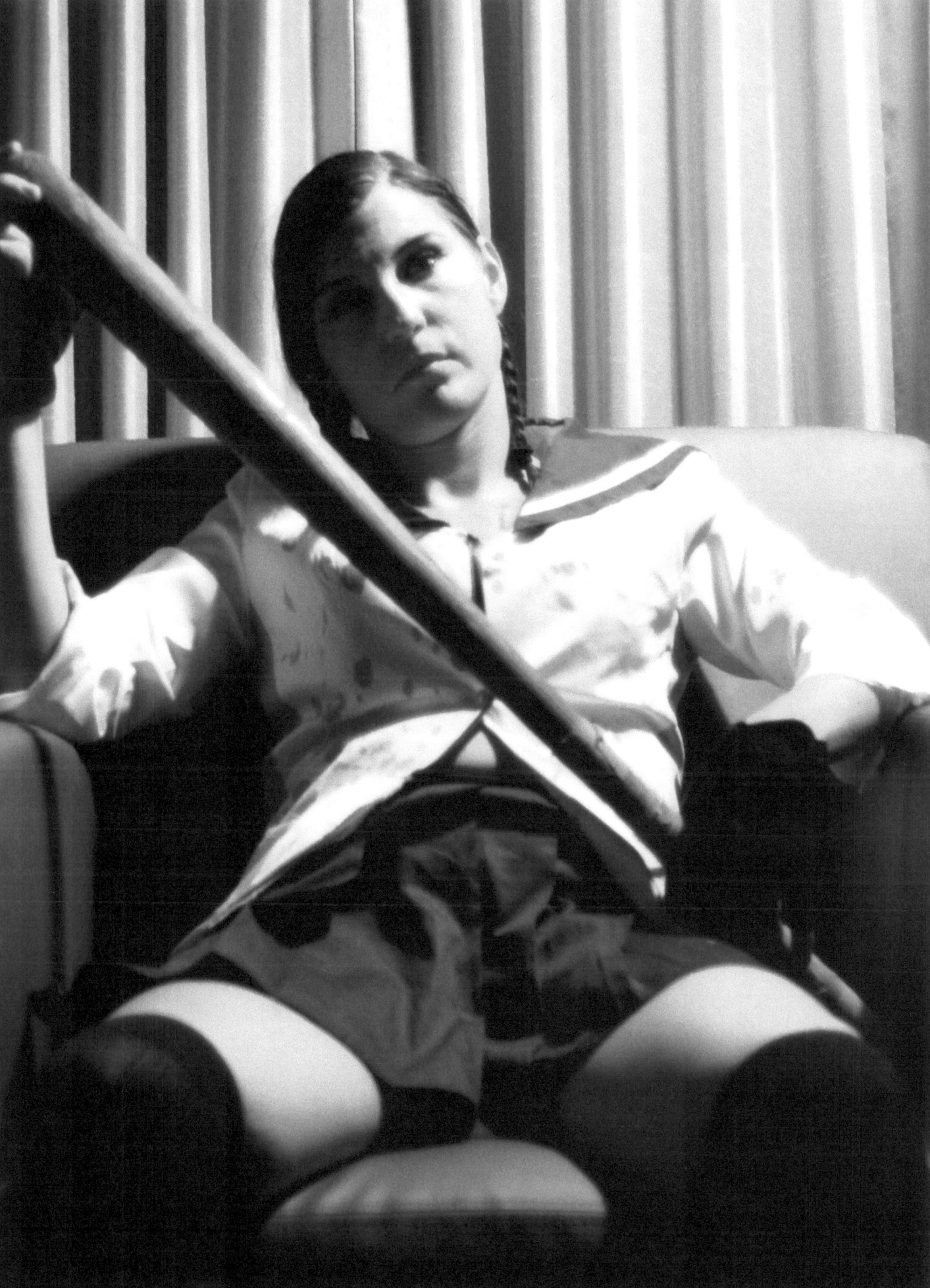

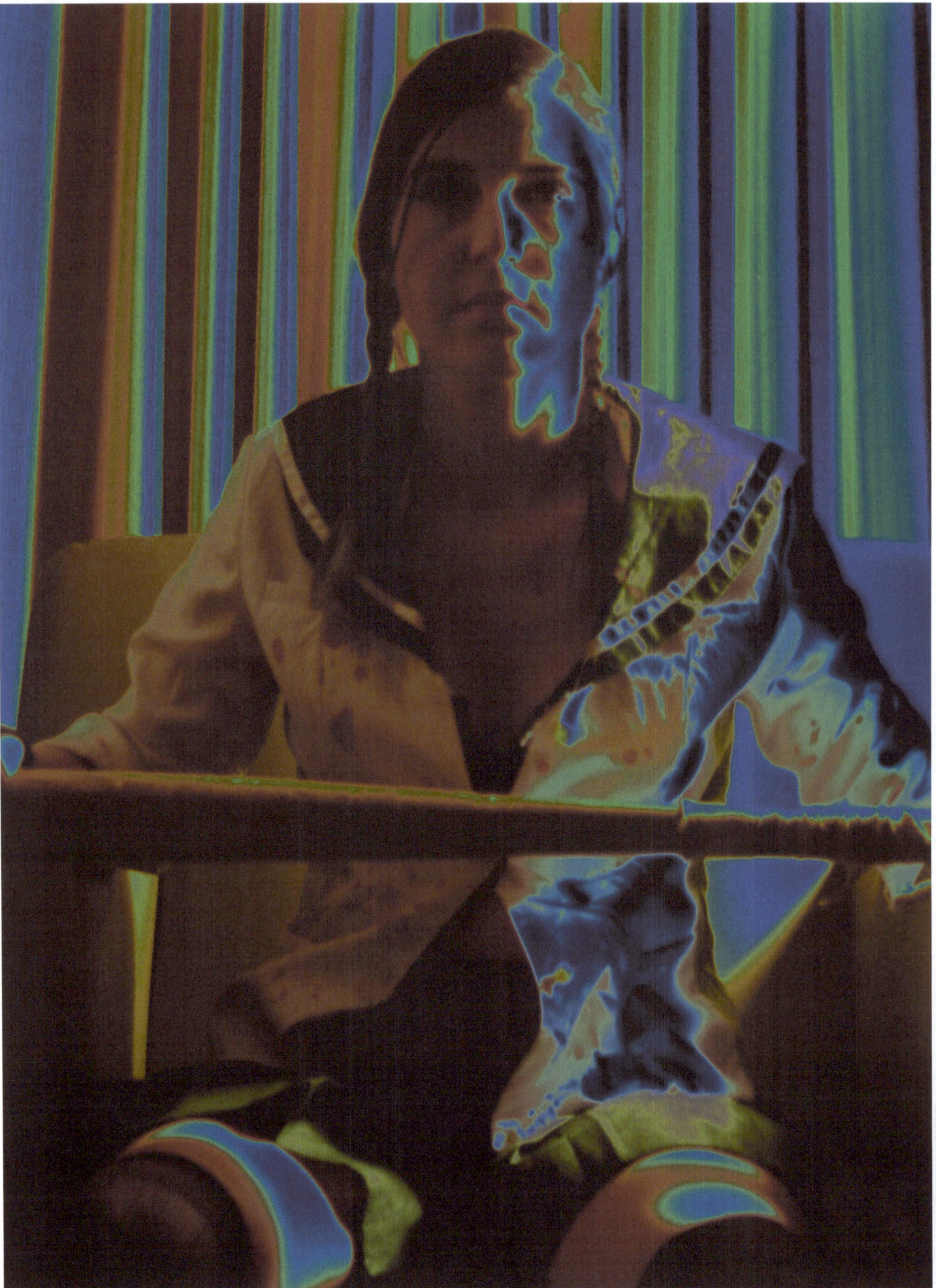

www.ingramcontent.com/pod-product-compliance
Lightning Source LLC
Chambersburg PA
CBHW050812180526
45159CB00004B/1643